Make It Happen

Make It Happen

Motivation and mindset to help you go from burnout to balance

Victoria Knowles-Lacks

There is a printable workbook to go along with this book. If you'd like to download a copy, visit
www.victoriaknowleslacks.com/workbook

Join the MAKE IT HAPPEN Facebook group
www.facebook.com/groups/makeithappenbook

Published by Victoria Knowles-Lacks

www.victoriaknowleslacks.com

© Copyright Victoria Knowles-Lacks

MAKE IT HAPPEN

ISBN 978-1-789-72226-0

Book formatted by www.bookformatting.co.uk

Contents

Dedication

In memory of the greatest man I ever knew,
Karl Heinz Lacks
1956-2017

Introduction

"Whether you think you can or whether you think you can't, you are right."
Henry Ford.

When you move out of your own way and stop telling yourself all of the reasons why you can't do something, amazing things start to happen. This is exactly what happened to me and this is exactly why I have written this book – to share with you, so you can do the same.

I wrote this book for you if you are ready to change your ways, step into a life you love, and to do the work to make it happen.

I totally know what it's like when you are stressed, burnt out and trying to do everything yourself. It is so hard and it feels never-ending. I know what it is like to struggle and know exactly how it feels for your world to come crashing down when you lose people you love. I also know that there is another way and that comes with changing your mindset.

Before I go on, I want to start by saying the most almighty and heartfelt thank you for your support, and I love that you are reading this. I honestly can't even begin to tell you how incredible it feels to have written a book. Seriously! I really hope you enjoy reading this book as much as I enjoyed writing it.

The purpose of me writing 'Make it Happen' is to share some of the incredible life and business lessons that I have learnt on my journey as an entrepreneur. The journey which has seen me go from burnout to balance, from stressed to calm. Balance feels great and I've managed to manoeuvre myself into a position that feels so good – a position which sees me work six hours a day, feel motivated, and even go on holiday without my laptop. I am in a place I didn't even know existed just a few short years ago.

I spent a lot of time with a scarcity mindset. I would tell myself I never had enough time, I never had enough money, I was never doing enough, I wasn't getting ahead enough. If you are now where I was then, it is my hope that this book will inspire you, and that you can make changes to your life.

What I am learning is that life is so much simpler than we make it out to be. We are so unbelievably capable and so many of us have a tendency to overcomplicate things (I put my hand up here), blow things out of proportion and talk ourselves out of doing things. When we take things for what they are, see the good and don't operate from a place of fear, we live incredible lives.

I can't recognise the person I was just a few years ago and I absolutely feel that I have been through a transformation. All it has taken is small but consistent actions and steps towards gaining a positive mindset every single day. Small but consistent shifts can and will 100% change your life. A morning routine has been at the core of the change, along with prioritising, fine-tuning my time, and utilising and creating productivity tools. I have put in place boundaries, streamlined my business processes and, every single day without fail, I spend time being intentional and grateful.

I genuinely believe that we can make anything happen and I am proof of that. Have I reached my full potential on what I can make happen yet? No way, I am only just getting started. Am I something special? Absolutely not. I am one of the most normal women I know. I just decided to put myself first and to focus on possibility instead of challenges.

What if everything you are going through, or have been through, is preparing you for what you want?

My story is one of following your heart, hitting rock bottom and building back up in a way that feels good. It is about letting go of what no longer serves you, getting some perspective and chasing down your best life in whatever shape or form that looks like to you.

INTRODUCTION

I have put my heart and soul into this three-part book, and I cannot wait for you to dive in. Part One is about me and my journey, which includes both success and struggle, plus lots more about me. I share my work addiction and the highs and lows of running a small but mighty business. I delve into the impact of having a terminally ill Father, and what I learnt from seeing him bravely face cancer, plus the turning points and transformations in my life.

In Part Two, I focus on mindset and share the exact steps and strategies I used, and still use every day, to create this momentous shift from busy to balanced. Having a positive approach and mindset has changed everything for me, from stepping into my power and potential, to getting over self doubt, and just getting out of my own way. When you start to see situations and challenges in a different way, you lose the 'impossible' and see 'possible'. Part Two has a workbook and lots of examples and tools and tips to help you get started.

Part Three features 'The Seven Principles of Balance'. I created these seven, action-based pillars for creating a streamlined, systemised and good feeling business which will enable you to live more and work less. Many of my coaching clients have applied these to their businesses too and have had the same results.

Only you have your gifts and only you can make your impact on the world. You just have to go and do it. Don't shy away, step into your power and go after exactly what it is you want. Share your message unapologetically, because everything can change in a moment You never know who needs to hear what you have to say.

If you need to hear this, then I wrote this book for you. You are far too special to be the only thing standing in your way.

All my love and gratitude.

Victoria x

Foreword

I knew right from the start that Victoria is an amazing person destined for greatness. Having watched her create an award winning business, whilst dealing with all manner of challenges, which would ultimately lead to her burning out. I couldn't be prouder of the woman she has become.

Eight years on from setting up that first company, Victoria changed an industry and started a movement and it was through her hard work, foresight and commitment that made it happen.

Being married to Victoria, I have seen her go from strength to strength and achieve some incredible things. Even when she has been at her lowest, her resolve and inner strength are unfaltering. She has had to overcome the most difficult and challenging time with the loss of her Dad, who meant so much to her. How she has used this life changing experience for good, and transform into the woman she is now, has been remarkable. Every day she inspires me.

Seeing first hand the shifts she has made in terms of her mindset and restructuring her business has been humbling. Not only has she changed her life, mine has changed too through her balance and beliefs.

Victoria writing this book has made me even more immensely proud of her, not to mention she did it all from start to finish within a year which is an amazing achievement in itself, whilst coping with grief and running her business. She is the ultimate person to make it happen, and I hope you enjoy her story as much as I have enjoyed living it with her.

FOREWORD

So now it's time for you to dive into her amazing story and reap the rewards this book will teach you!

All the best,

Keiran – Victoria's Lucky Husband

Heartfelt Love and Acknowledgements

First up, to my amazing family for their unconditional love, help and advice in writing this book. For the endless proofreading, grammar checking and general support in making this book a reality. I literally could not have done it without them and I know I drove them mad.

To my amazing Mum, Janet, for everything she has done for me and my sisters. For being such a wonderful Mum to us all.

Jan – you are stronger than you know and you inspire us all so much.

My amazing sisters, Anna, Caroline and Rosie for the love, the banter and just being themselves.

The most insane amounts of love to my darling and handsome husband Keiran. This man has believed in me, kept me going, supported me, nurtured me and picked up the pieces when I was broken.

To Grandma Phyllis for being the strongest, most incredible woman and for raising such an incredible son. We love you!

To the rest of the Lacks and Knowles families for their love and banter.

To my S&CBC girls, past and present – there are far too many of you to mention. Know that I am grateful to each and every one of you. Without your love and support I wouldn't be here now and together we have achieved so much.

To my Squad, my besties, The S&CBC and LSC Members, and anyone who has believed in me or supported me over the years. You are all part of it and you are why I am doing this.

PART 1
MY STORY

Chapter 1

The Struggle Was Real

This girl was on fire! On the surface I had it all and I was the luckiest person I knew. I had married the man of my dreams, my family were all well, my six-figure events business was hugely successful and continued to grow at an incredible rate. I had it all and was on top of my game.

I had become well-known and well-respected in my industry, people knew who I was (which in itself was such a great feeling). At my events, women would tell me I was changing their lives (crazy, I know!). I would be at industry events and people I respected congratulated me on what I was achieving. It was staggering. I was also really lucky to receive letters and emails of thanks on a near constant basis, and each one meant so much to me; it was phenomenal. I had managed to disrupt a male-dominated industry and, more importantly, I had created an impact on women – women just like me. That impact came through creating a community, confidence and camaraderie.

I want to tell you how grateful I am that you have picked up my book. It has been such a journey to get to this point and I have learnt so much about myself in the process, so I really hope you enjoy it. Before I get stuck in, I want to tell you a little more about me. I am 35 and live in a village on the Worcestershire/Shropshire border in the UK with my gorgeous husband, Keiran and our elderly Lakeland Terrier, Rocket. I love the countryside, the beach and basically just being outside in the sunshine, and the sense of freedom and possibility that brings. I am on a real journey to be the best I can be in all areas of my life. I love to help others and to share what I have learnt. I believe that everything happens to us for a reason, and that things happen for us and not to us. I am massively passionate about sharing what I have learnt about life, mindset, small business and designing a life I love!

I like to think of myself as kind-hearted and fortunate, yet ambitious and committed to my cause. I am very lucky to have clarity and to know who I am and where I am heading. I have a real ability to join the dots on things and to see a clear route to the bigger picture. Throughout my journey, I have learnt to make my dreams bigger than my fears, and to keep my sense of humour throughout. I know there is always a way out of everything, and I can find the good in most situations.

My hope is that, by sharing the incredible rollercoaster I have been on, it will inspire you to make the changes you need to in your life. Whatever your situation is, I genuinely believe that there is always another way. That, and when you change your mindset, your life changes too. I know this because, when I started to change my mindset, everything else just seemed to fall into place. My life just felt more straightforward and I let go of so much which was no longer serving me. I have a ton of valuable lessons to share with you that I have learnt over the past few years, which I will share in the coming chapters.

There are so many parts to my story. Seriously, I could write an entire collection of books on the things that I have done, or that have happened to me. In this book, however, I am going to focus on: business, balance, family, grief and moving forward, even when you feel like you cannot. To me, my journey has been about making it happen, doing the work and going from an unsustainable place where my business ran me, to a place where my business fits around my life.

Before we get into it, I want to share one important lesson I learnt in my struggle, which is that there is always another way. No matter what we are struggling with, or how never-ending it feels, there is always another way. We just have to find it.

In my life now I have the time and space to focus on what is important to me. I have cut away the hardship I created for myself, the triviality, and the struggle. If I can do it, you can too. And I am going to show you how.

Let's get going. I set up my first business, The Shotgun & Chelsea Bun Club (which I will refer to as the S&CBC) in September 2011. It was one of those evolutions and those accidental hobby-turned-businesses; the ones fuelled by passion that snowball in the most unimaginable and unexpected of ways!

From that one September day in 2011, with a lot of hard work and all the emotions in between, I took the S&CBC from a dream to the largest all-women shooting club in Europe. A shooting club with a global reach and members as far afield as Europe, North America and Australia. I never dared to dream of how incredible or far-reaching it would be, or how just a girl like me could create a community that would go on to change an industry and, more importantly, lives.

Right now, I want to tell you a little more about the S&CBC and set the scene, so you can get a better understanding of how it works and a feel for the dynamics of the club, as this plays a role later on in the book.

The focus of the S&CBC is to bring non-shooting women into the sport in a really fun and supportive way, also to provide a place for more experienced shooters to network and make friends. Shooting is rather male-dominated and, when you don't have that 'in', it can be so daunting to get started, or at least it was when I set up the S&CBC. My plan was to make the sport really accessible and attractive, and create events that I'd love to go to.

I am so proud of the massive impact I have made on an industry and on the lives of so many. It really isn't just about shooting, it is so much more than that. We run some one hundred introduction to clay shooting events a year all over England. Alongside this, we have an incredible community around the events, where countless lifelong friendships have been formed. We are well known at home and abroad for our fun and supportive vibe that has put women's shooting on the map. S&CBC events are held at professional shooting schools, who provide us with facilities and instructors. We promote them as S&CBC events and bring the fun (and the cake!).

At the events, we start with a big welcome and safety brief, before all of the women head off in groups of six to the shooting ground with an instructor. The ladies are coached over different targets and they shoot for around two hours in their groups, and then it's time to reconvene as one big group for tea and cake (hence the Chelsea Bun part of the name!). It is all about fun, confidence and community!

Alongside the events, we have a brilliant membership. I have met and made friends with some of the most incredible women! I have also seen the most incredible transformations within some of our members too. Every now and then, we have women who are nervous coming to events and they try their absolute hardest not to run back to the car, or hide in the loo, as it is so far out of their comfort zone! Only a few months later, they will return, decked out with all the kit, their own shotguns, confidence, and new friends! To me, this is what it is all about!

The S&CBC has grown so much and, in Summer 2018, I 'franchised' out the events. I now have a strong team of six wonderful women who run the S&CBC's separate geographical regions. They are doing incredible things for the club and really driving it forward. I can't even tell you how good it feels to be so well-supported, and it is a privilege to have so many great women around me – both in the team and in the community.

Prior to the S&CBC there were, of course, many amazing women shooters leading the way and some incredible role models for us girls, but no real 'women's shooting industry' as we have now. In a few short years after The Shotgun & Chelsea Bun Club started, the whole women's shooting scene exploded. The industry responded and it is incredible – long may it continue!

With the S&CBC I created my own niche, a niche that bought some incredible women into my world. Over the years I have been lucky enough to have support from so many women, shooting grounds, and companies. They have all been a part of the journey and helped to grow the club to where it is today, and I could not have done it without them. It has been such a team effort, and it is so humbling when people help like they have helped me. As I write this, I can literally feel my heart brimming with pride!

Since the S&CBC was founded, we have provided a route into shooting for nearly 20,000 women (and counting). This has to be my proudest achievement – me, Victoria, from Worcestershire, with no experience in marketing, has welcomed over 20,000 women to her events! I also created 'National Ladies' Shooting Day' which is the world's largest, all female clay shooting event – it is pretty epic what you can achieve when you put your mind to it, isn't it? The S&CBC has also won ten awards, plus I got a special honour for my services to the sport. I have been on TV twice, we have been featured in the national and international press many times, I've done several national radio interviews, a magazine even called me a "pioneer".

I was literally smashing it – or so everyone thought…

The thing is, not everything is always as it seems and you only know what people tell you. It's so easy to think that people are absolutely winning at life and everything is perfect for them, especially in this Instagram age when we curate a beautiful front end to our life, regardless of what's happening behind the scenes!

I want to be brutally honest with you. You might look at me and think *"It's ok for you Victoria, you've got it all figured out and your life looks perfect"* and that's ok. I want to share with you what I call my 'struggle' in hope of it inspiring you and if you are in the struggle, if you are in a similar place, I want to give you some hope to find another way.

In the early years of the S&CBC, behind the scenes, it wasn't great. In fact, it was really dire. I loved what I did but at times I couldn't see the wood for the trees and I was stressed in a big way.

Back then in my years of struggle I had no balance, clarity, or structure and, on occasions, I was totally winging it and just hoping for the best. I am sure those are precisely the traits you want someone writing a business book to have! To say I struggled in the early years is an understatement. There were times when I felt as though I was on an out of control rollercoaster in the dark, not knowing where the next stomach-churning drop or jolting turn would be.

Looking back, I remember I felt anxious so much of the time and everything felt so difficult, impossible even. I often just felt like the tough times would never end and this was my life, which is really sad as really it was all totally unnecessary, I was just very inexperienced and I had my mindset wrong. Of course, now I know different – I love a bit of hindsight!

TRUTH BOMB: No matter how tough things are, you are tougher and you will always get through it because you have to

Before I go into the details of why and how I struggled, if you are in one right now, know that it will end soon. I know full well how awful it is when everything seems impossible, you have to know that you will grow and be challenged in ways you thought weren't possible, but you will come out of it the other side stronger, clearer, more empowered and able to do anything.

Since mine ended, I have manoeuvred myself into a position where I have more free time than work time, and I feel good 90% of the time. Please note, yes, I still have days where I feel lousy / rubbish / annoyed etc, even me! My life has ease, flow and so much 'me time' – three things which I lacked and craved for so long.

The Struggle

The struggle began in 2012, the year after I started my business. It happened because I was so inexperienced and naive and I thought if I just worked hard, it would all be ok. I didn't really give a second thought to my health, my relationships and happiness, all I knew was that I wanted to keep the S&CBC growing. I wanted to bring as many women in to the sport as I could. I had so much passion and enthusiasm, but the problem was that I lacked structure, a clear vision, any kind of boundaries and I didn't really have a clue on how to prioritise my business operations. These are all fundamental things in order to lead a successful and sustainable business.

The S&CBC was growing fast, really fast and, towards the end of 2012, and for the whole of 2013 and 2014, I was exhausted. I felt as though I was being pulled in a million different directions and I completely burnt out a few times, too – more on that later. I'd become relentless to the detriment of my family, my body, and my life outside of my business. I was always busy, it was a joke... I was pulling 14 hour days most days, I wasn't eating well and was just filling up on sugar and carbs to get me through the day. I never took time off and I could not stop working.

Like many entrepreneurs, I wore 'busy' as a badge of honour, and I thought that was how it should be. It actually makes me cringe so much looking back. My favourite topic of conversation was always how busy I was, literally I was like a slow, stuck and really boring record. Just to illustrate my point (this is embarrassing...), I often receive reminders in my Facebook memories saying things like "*153 emails done, 86 to go!*" Can you even imagine having me as a friend / wife / sister / daughter? I must have been hell and I have no idea how people put up with me! I'm so grateful to everyone who stuck with me, despite how intense (and irritating) I must have been!

I had my struggle so ingrained in my mind that I couldn't even keep my laptop closed on my birthday, Christmas, or any other day of significance.

An example, in October 2013, my darling Grandad, Roland died. It was the first death of someone in my immediate family, and he had been such a huge part of my life. On the morning of his funeral, instead of being with my Grandma and supporting her, I was working. It's so sad isn't it? I couldn't see past my laptop screen, or out of the S&CBC bubble, which was my life. I started to loathe who I was becoming.

Things became a lot worse too. I want to give you some context and tell you about my struggle, as it's a big part of my story. I don't want to bring you down with my former woes, as that isn't what this book is about, in fact I wrote it in hope of inspiring you – but equally, I want to let you know what it was like and to set the scene. There is so much I could tell you, so I am going to summarise a few things that kept me in that place of struggle.

Some particularly low points along my journey:

- Lack of structure. I knew what I wanted to achieve, but I didn't plan anything in as much detail as I should have. I had a vague idea and I just did it. Taking action for the sake of it is exhausting and the long way round.
- Having a real victim mindset. I was the victim of busy and I just kept telling myself that, so that's what I kept getting more of.
- Not looking after myself. I didn't even know self-love or self-care were a thing, and I prioritised work over sleep and my health and wellbeing. You have to put yourself first.
- Putting my business above all else, including my family for the first few years. I can't get that time back.
- Not having boundaries and being fully available 24/7. I didn't have the confidence to just leave it and reply to emails when it suited me. I felt as though I had to reply to people there and then, even when they didn't expect it.
- Not putting my phone away, ever. Sleeping with it on, next to my bed. Looking at every single notification that came in.
- For feeling that, if I wasn't actually engaged working at that moment, I was failing. My self-worth was absolutely tied to my work.
- Working 14 hours per day and being away over 40+ weekends a year is insane, unnecessary and actually ridiculous. If I had some structure, I could have achieved all I did without being tied to my laptop.
- There were people who wanted to see me fail. They ran me down in the lowest of ways and at the time, I let it get to me and distract me. Now I know they were just reflecting their insecurities onto me and

they had problems with themselves.

- Working with friends and not having set guidelines or scope were some stressful times, when we were both at cross purposes. Having to navigate unnecessary fallouts was sad, stressful, and avoidable.
- Not having the right systems – or, in fact – any systems in place. For too long, I battled on with spreadsheets and out of sync files, creating so much more work for myself.
- Not charging what I was worth in the early days. The lack of self-confidence took me to the brink a few times financially.
- Not having the courage sometimes to speak up, and to let people guide me to suit their agenda.
- I struggled with confidence a fair bit. I struggled with putting myself out there, in my pricing, and in asking for help. I stalled because of my lack of confidence.
- Multitasking – working on about ten different things at once – meant that nothing ever really had my full attention, so it seems as though nothing was ever completed to the best of my ability.

That's a lot, isn't it? I feel tired just listing all that and it was all from my own life. When I look back over those points and the other things which have happened, I feel an equal mix of sadness for the former me and pride that I powered through it all and came out the other side a better person. They say when it rains it pours and I had a lot of the above points going on simultaneously. Also, putting your business over everything and everyone you love will ultimately come back and bite you and is a recipe for regret and, to me, regret is one of the worst feelings you can have.

When I quit my 9 to 5 job, my vision wasn't to work 24/7, but I just couldn't stop for some reason. I would find myself sending tweets or replying to emails when I had a rare minute to go to the loo. When I was out with friends, my mind was always on my business and I was never really present. I'd visit my Grandma and frequently sneak off to check bookings. My passion and my zest for business had become an unhealthy obsession.

The sad reality was that I was already so far ahead, I just couldn't see it at the time. I didn't really ever stop to take a moment to appreciate and look back on how far I had come, and the impact I had already made. I guess looking back I just thought people were being kind to me to make me feel better, isn't that sad? I feel like I want to reach out to the former me for a hug and a bit of a shake!

During my struggle, I had no idea about systems, automation, boundaries, protecting my time and energy, or self-care. I also had no idea about perspective. All I knew was that I had to keep going and to keep quieting the nagging feeling that I was out of my depth. Like a lot of first-time business owners, I did absolutely everything myself to start with. I didn't seem to ever learn the easy way, and I don't think I ever considered delegation as an option. Can you get a feel for what my life was like?

TRUTH BOMB: Asking for help when you need it is an act of kindness to yourself

I loved the challenge of learning everything in my business but, in my quest for progress, I cut corners. My business felt chaotic and I was burning out. I am talking full-on emotional burnout, to the point of exhaustion. Burnout which kept me on the sofa or in bed for several days. There were days when I was broken, and I was physically so exhausted and drained that I couldn't even get out of bed, I did that to myself. There is no way any of us would ever expect what I put myself through from anyone else, so I have no idea why I thought it was ok to do it to myself. In Chapter Three, I want to tell you how I turned this burnout into transformation, and how I got off the treadmill and changed my ways once and for all.

Through my lowest points, and there were plenty, my family and friends were so good and supportive to me and the incredible S&CBC spirit pulled me through. My family listened to my woes, nourished me and propped me up as much as I'd allow them. Then, there were my members, I have an amazing group of girls who became my best friends. They rallied round to help me, and hosted events for me as they knew what I was going through, and they kept me going too. They would take the strain and pressure off me and afford me a weekend at home with Keiran to just chill. I have no idea what I would have done without these girls who gave me some time back. I owe them such a lot and I have no doubt the S&CBC would have ceased if it wasn't for them. There's that phrase "When women support women incredible things happen", I honestly can't agree with this more as I was so supported and incredible things were happening.

So, there was a lot of seemingly endless work and a lot of stress going on. When I thought it couldn't get any worse, it did. I hit an all-time low when, in late 2012, my incredible Dad, Karl was diagnosed with Stage 4 bowel cancer.

Like a lot of girls, I can't even begin to put into words how much l loved my Dad. He was such a hero and he took it all in his stride, just like he did with anything difficult. He was a pillar of strength. Like all amazing Dads, he told us not to worry but, of course, my Mum, sisters, and I were all devastated. On top of my 'busy' mindset and my ever mounting to-do list, I felt stunned and just numb.

TRUTH BOMB: Don't take anything for granted, because it can all change in a moment

I remember hearing his words, *"I've got cancer love,"* but not really knowing how to process it. My reaction was to keep working. I guess it was a coping mechanism. After the cancer news, I made an effort to see my parents more, but I always had my laptop with me and I'd always be working. I was kind of present, but might as well not have been as my focus was on my business.

A few months after being diagnosed, my Dad had an operation to remove the tumour from his bowel. Thankfully, all went to plan and that was that. At the time, though, I was away at a shoot when he was in hospital, so I didn't go and see him. In my head, the thought of taking a few hours out of my day was too big a price to pay. How bad is that?

In all fairness to myself, over the coming months, I was filling events up and the S&CBC was growing fast. Magic was starting to happen and the club was gaining massive momentum. Events were selling out, I launched a membership and I felt like I was really getting the club out there. I was proud, but at the same time I still felt like I was addicted to work and sinking.

I set up the S&CBC as I wanted to make clay shooting as accessible to as many women as possible. To do this, I kept my price point for events low, which meant that margins were super tight. This added a ton of pressure to the mix and meant that I had money troubles on top of my business troubles, and now my Dad's cancer.

I think it's really important to talk about money as so many of us have struggled with it. Plus, I am a big believer in the power of our stories and you never know who needs to hear yours. I want to share with you my first major financial breakdown, because if you are where I was, then I hope it helps.

The meltdown came on Christmas Eve, 2014 – of all the days… I remember sitting on my sofa in tears as I only had £28 left of my business overdraft. I was on the verge of bankruptcy, it was Christmas, and I hadn't bought any presents. I remember just feeling this overwhelming sadness and feeling like an absolute failure. I had blown it.

I'd got to this place as I didn't organise any events that December and January, as I knew I needed a rest and some serious downtime. It was that year I had to go VAT registered, and I had such a pain with it too. With my quarterly VAT payments wiping me out, and the lack of events, I had effectively choked my income.

That Christmas Eve, I felt so sorry for myself, it really was the lowest of the low, and as if I had totally spiralled out of control. One thing my Dad always taught me though, and that was to never give up.

So after a few solid hours of self pity I stopped feeling sorry for myself, got my act together, accepted where I was and vowed to get back up and turn it around. On Boxing Day, I did a membership promo and got about 30 new members, in the New Year I put on some new events which helped cash flow and I chalked the whole thing down to experience.

While it was a stressful situation to be in, and I know money troubles can feel suffocating, I know now that being so broke taught me resilience, creative thinking, and courage. Like all difficult situations, we go through them and we grow through them. It really taught me how to hold my nerve and that the end is only the end if we let it be. With situations where we feel defeated but don't give up, we nearly always come out stronger the other side. Just like the phrase 'Sometimes you win, sometimes you learn'. I definitely learnt that time and I now know that this is what it's all about – learning.

That Christmas, I took some time off to be with my Mum, Dad, sisters, and Keiran. It felt good and almost as though it had shocked me into focussing on what was important. I had a blissful week of just being with my family and, for the first time in a long time, being present. It was a shame that it had to come to this to have that week, but I am a big believer that everything happens for a reason. Sometimes, seemingly unfair things happen and they seem nonsensical at the time, especially when you are trying your best and giving it your all. Ultimately though, nothing is ever that bad and this was my first dose of perspective, something which I needed so badly. I made a promise to myself, from that day, that I would never go back to financial rock bottom and I haven't.

Hopefully you've got an idea of how bad things were, and how wrong my mindset was. I hope you can see how I'd created all this unnecessary chaos and undue stress around myself. I had adopted a scarcity mindset and I kept telling myself I didn't have enough time and so that meant I never had enough. I had lost who I was under layers and layers of negative limiting beliefs.

On the plus side, the layer upon layer of self-limiting, restrictive habits and beliefs I had are now long gone and they've been replaced with possibility, balance and doing what's right for me. I think it's really important to highlight that being constantly busy is not cool, dashing around and running yourself into the ground isn't cool at all. When you are focussed on 'busy' instead of progress, you will feel like enough is never enough and it never will be.

As time went on, my friends, members, and family rallied around and got me through my struggles. They shouldered some of the burden with me (it was a burden and it was killing me). Seriously, I have no idea what I would have done without them. My Mum took over doing membership renewals which was a massive help, and my friends hosted events and helped with admin. I relinquished total control and let people help me. These girls, they know who they are, totally saved me and the S&CBC!

To close this chapter I want to share with you a few key points I learnt when I was in my struggle:

1. Balance is key. You must have balance; not enough and you are stressed, too much and you are not focussed.
2. You can't do your best work if you are worn out and not looking after yourself.
3. When you change your mindset, you can change your life.
4. Your self-worth comes from within you. It has nothing to do with how busy you are, how much content you are putting out, or how many social media likes you receive.
5. When you step up, people might want to gun you down. It's not your problem, it's theirs.
6. You can get through anything and there is always another way.
7. Setting up the appropriate boundaries and systems early on is essential.
8. Let people help you if they want to. Your friends don't want to see you struggle, so take them up on offers to help – it's as much for them as it is for you.
9. There is a huge difference between busy and productive.
10. Put a realistic deadline on everything. It is amazing how quickly you can complete tasks.

Chapter 2

In Case You are Wondering Who I Am

I want to kick this off with five things that I love:

- Summer mornings and long, sunny walks with my dog.
- People who try, even when they don't have a clue.
- Travelling. Put me on a long-haul flight to somewhere hot and I'm in my element.
- A beautiful notebook and my fountain pen.
- A Netflix marathon with Keiran on the sofa, with a bottle of fizz and a box of chocolates.

My struggles in Chapter 1 are way behind me now, thank goodness. It's funny as I can't really recognise or even relate to my old self, which is bizarre really, but in a good way. Now I feel balanced, focussed, and strong and I love so much about my life because I have designed it how I want it, and I have done the work to get it there. I work for six hours a day and, if I need to take a day off, I do so without stressing about it. When my laptop lid is closed, I mentally check out of work and that work obsession is long gone. My business is set up in a way that affords me space and I'm definitely more aligned with my purpose these days.

Because I changed my outlook, everything has changed. Gone is the scarcity mindset and in its place is one of abundance and possibility. I am travelling a lot more, my relationships are better than ever, I am exercising a lot more, and I am nourishing myself as I never have before and I feel good! This feeling seemed way out of reach for so long and at one point probably impossible. If you are struggling right now, then I hope my story will give you the inspiration you need to keep pushing on, just like I did. You always have to keep going.

I am naturally curious and I love to know more about people, so I'm going to share some of my background and upbringing with you, just because I love to know as much about other people – I always think it's nice to know about people and to get to know them.

My Family

I am one of four sisters and the second eldest. There's Anna who's the eldest, then me, then Caroline, then Rosie, the baby. My sisters and I are all so different, yet all so similar. We are the ultimate girl squad. There's lots of banter, occasional squabbling amongst ourselves but we're all as thick as thieves, and we're always there for each other, no matter what.

I want to just take a moment to say I know exactly how lucky we are to have each other. I know full well that not everyone is as fortunate as us to have siblings, especially ones so close and funny (we all think we're hilarious!...).

My parents are the best. Karl, my Dad, a tall, strong, also hilariously funny, worldly wise man with infinite wisdom and the most beautiful, big heart. Janet, my Mum is a lioness and one of life's real sweethearts. She's so kind and gentle, but has a hilarious sense of humour! Laughter and silliness are a big part of our family lives and there's a lot of it, I adore my family so much. Then of course there's my darling Keiran, the man who deserves a medal for sticking with me through everything. He makes me proud every day.

My parents were such great role models; a testament to love, hard work and happiness.

We didn't have a lot growing up, but what we lacked in finances we more than made up for in love. We had really loving, stable and supportive parents, for this, I am so grateful. Our house was filled with love My parents gave my sisters and I so much.

Growing up, I was the ultimate free-range kid and I had a real sense of freedom (which I still have now) and I was always out in the countryside. At age eight, I was always out on my bike or spending time with our ponies and just doing as I pleased! My parents knew I was worldly-wise from a young age, so they just let me go out and explore.

My Dad worked long hours in factories to support us all, until later, when he fulfilled his dream of being a property developer. He had a real knack for it and I have such fun memories of helping him knock down walls and paint stuff!

My Mum stayed home and raised us. I literally have no idea how my parents managed to stay sane and cope with us. To say we were a handful, is probably another massive understatement! It was tough for them, but they never showed it. I think out of all of us, I was the biggest pain and most strong willed! I knew I had a fierce spirit and expensive tastes. An example of this was Cliff. Cliff was a stunning 16.2hh thoroughbred ex-racehorse that I'd managed to negotiate with my parents to let me have. They thought they were getting me a pony but, through my excellent negotiation skills, what I ended up getting was a stunning high-maintenance, highly spirited ex-racehorse. He wasn't particularly safe and he cost my parents a fortune, but he was my pride and joy.

Growing up

From an early age I showed entrepreneurial spirit and I was keen to pay my way. When I was ten years old, I had a regular round of cars to wash and odd jobs to do for neighbours. I had a paper round too. At thirteen, I got my first job at a boatyard, cleaning canal boats – gruelling work for just £10 for a full day, but it gave me some money of my own, some independence and I could contribute a bit to housekeeping.

Going into my teenage years, that fierce spirit carried on and I was brave. I always had a feeling I'd go on and do something different to my school friends, but I never really knew what it would be. I didn't think I was any better than my peers; I just knew I was different to them. I couldn't cope with the thought of mediocrity and I had this fire inside me, but I could never really pinpoint what it was burning for.

I never really knew what I wanted to do when I grew up. You know how some people know exactly what they want to do? This wasn't me and I literally had no idea so I took a year out. I went to horseracing college for a while as it seemed like a smart thing to do after I'd had a quite serious riding accident. It was fun, but it wasn't me, so I did what all unsure teenagers do – I went to Ibiza for the summer and partied! I was big into house music at the time and I had such a wild child summer in Ibiza, and was so into it that I went back again the following summer, which is a whole different book in itself! When I returned from Ibiza for the second time I moved to London to study at London College of Fashion. It was fun and I liked the buzz of London and I loved the nights out and the feeling of opportunity, but I never felt like I could settle. Plus, Fashion School was just a little too pretentious for me, I liked it, but my heart just wasn't in it so I went home.

Work Wise

In 2004, my next chapter took me to Australia for a working holiday with my sister, Caroline. We landed ourselves dream jobs as cowgirls rounding cattle up on horseback on a ranch in the outback. It was the most fun! We had endless freedom, fresh air, and were outside all day long, we wore cowboy boots, rode all day, and drank beer in the evenings and we were literally living our best lives. We also had occasional trips to the city for which we applied some makeup, wore high heels, and went out drinking just to keep us sane. The ultimate balance!

Part of me wanted to stay in Australia, but we did the right thing and came home in early 2007. Our Dad was having major surgery to have both of his hips replaced and, deep down, we missed our family. We have the best memories, and being away taught us so much and Caroline and I still recount our travels on a regular basis. We really made the most of it!

When we returned home, our parents had moved to a beautiful little village, which we loved. There was an awesome local pub and a real sense of community spirit. It was around this time that I discovered clay shooting – a brand-new hobby outside of horses, house music and gin and tonics; a hobby which would go on to change everything.

That winter felt bleak, part of me still felt as though I couldn't really settle and there was always this nagging feeling of not knowing what I wanted to do. During that long, miserable winter, part of me wanted to go back to London to do the fashion thing, so I did some work experience with Fashion PR agencies and with some designers. It just wasn't for me, though and I didn't really fit in, and it just never felt right, so I came home again.

There were three things I knew I wanted out of life for sure:

1. to make my Mum and Dad proud
2. to make an impact
3. and to have freedom

Over ten years on, this is exactly what I have achieved although, looking back, it wasn't via the expected route. It's funny how things turn out, isn't it!

We had been back from Australia for about two months and I'd done a bit of temporary work, but I didn't feel aligned with anything. Everything just felt really dull compared to Australia (again scarcity mindset), until our next move. Our next move was quite amusing! Caroline and I went to a party one night and bumped into an old friend. He was hilarious and always really good fun. Slightly drunk, we told him how we both needed to get a job as we'd just got back home from travelling. He offered us a job on the spot and insisted, even though he was drunk, that he wanted both of us to work with him.

He was serious and the promise of a weekly wage, working in the countryside and not having to rely on Mum and Dad was tempting. We were in! After many gin and tonics, we hadn't really asked him what we'd be doing. I just assumed it would be marketing or some kind of admin.

Note: If you are accepting a job offer, always clarify what it is that you'll be doing.

I wish we had camera phones back then and that someone had taken a photo of my face when we pulled up to start work. Our friend greeted us with a pair of overalls and rigger boots! We didn't actually know that he had a welding company and that our job was to weld skips! It was hilarious and we soon got into it! It took two men one whole day to weld one skip. We had to cut the rusty bottoms and a bit of the sides out with a gas cutter and weld it all back together with a new bottom and sides. Caroline and I – as always – got stuck in and excelled in our new jobs. We bashed out two skips a day. Plus, we were epic at driving a forklift truck. So funny!

The welding was fun and we enjoyed it, but after three months of broken nails, spark burns and being constantly grubby, we were done. Then, out of nowhere, an amazing job working for a country house estate agency landed right in my lap. This was it and I really felt as though I was in my groove. I loved the job, I loved the people I worked with and I took so much pride in my work. I had just met my amazing, now husband Keiran (my absolute rock), I was shooting well and we'd just got our dog Rocket – life was good!

Then, the 2008 recession hit and I was made redundant from that job fairly sharpish. I was gutted. Over the next few months, I worked at some seriously uninspiring temporary jobs. This was probably the most unfulfilling time of my life. I remember feeling really down on my luck, but every day I tried to get a better job. Then in 2009, I got my job in Compliance with a Housing Association (the one I left in 2012 to follow my dreams). I enjoyed the work to begin with and my boss was hilarious, but it just wasn't me. I couldn't cope with the office gossip, petty rules and the mundaneness of everything. I knew for a while that I had to get out, and my soul was dying there. The only real plus points with the job were that it was well paid, I had flexi time, a lot of leave and a brilliant assistant. I did try and leave, but my wonderful boss coerced me back with a major pay rise. Of course, I took the money, which was great for a few months, until I felt like I was withering away again.

TRUTH BOMB: Money isn't everything, but it helps. If you are working in a job that kills your soul, then it's just not worth it

In late 2010, I started a blog to keep me sane. I loved clay shooting and thought starting a blog would allow me to keep focussed on shooting. Plus it was such a good distraction from the mediocrity of my day job.

The idea of my blog was to educate women who were interested in getting into shooting. I'd do write ups about my shooting trips, write gun and shooting clothing reviews, share recipes and so on. It really lit me up and provided an escape. It allowed me to be creative and I could put some of my heart and soul into it.

As the months went on, I grew a small Twitter following and started to get some positive momentum. People would ask me to guest blog for them and I started to get free clothes to review. Without realising it though, I had started to build a profile. I used to get up at 4:30 am to write blogs before work and then I'd spend my lunch breaks brainstorming future posts. It kept me nicely distracted from the boredom of my day job. I loved having this little side gig! The only reason I did the blog was because I loved doing it; I didn't really see it becoming a career.

The Start

I had a start in terms of gaining a very small audience, then the next piece to slot into place was the first event. On 26th September 2011, my life was about to change in the most extraordinary way – and I didn't even realise.

That was the day I took four girlfriends clay shooting. They weren't keen about it, and had all sorts of preconceptions about shooting. So I made a cake to lure them along, which of course worked a treat. We had a group shooting lesson and then we shot some clays. Afterwards, we had tea and cake in a little cabin, and we were all on such a high and excitedly re-lived the experience. It felt amazing to introduce my friends – who hadn't shot before – into a sport that I loved. It was a feeling I was keen to recreate.

Little did I know that clay shooting and cake would not only change my life, but the life of thousands of other women; not to mention the ripple effect that it would go on to create in the industry.

TRUTHBOMB: Never underestimate the significance of a single moment

Like many good things, my change in direction happened purely by accident. From that day, I knew I had stumbled across what I was meant to do, and I had found my calling. I finally felt aligned, I knew this because of the incredible enthusiasm I had – something had clicked within me. I knew I was going to create a community for women around clay shooting and cake. Sounds crazy, I know. If you think your niche is bizarre, then I hope I've inspired you!

Once I returned from the shoot, still high from all the sugar and adrenaline, I wrote a blog. I shared some photos, and told my readers about the incredible day I'd had and shared it on Twitter. Then the Tweets started. That day and the following days, I received several messages from women saying that they'd love to try shooting, but didn't know how. I also received messages from guys saying, *"Can my wife/sister/girlfriend come to one of your events?"*

"My events!" I loved how that felt and sounded and, in that moment, I knew what I needed to do. It's funny how things just happen and evolve when you don't force them and just let them unfold naturally. Innocent little things can change the course of your life. Sometimes when we can't see a way forward, situations just evolve and events happen that can improve things for us, if we can just wait. This was a classic example.

This was my way out of my soul-sucking job. I had finally found my purpose in life. I can't even tell you how good it felt that something had finally clicked. Years of not knowing what I wanted to do were over.

I knew it would be bigger than me and it wasn't just about guns and cake. It was recreating that feeling my friends and I'd had. It was about creating confidence and making new connections. I knew I was going into the business of empowerment and I was ready for it!

I knew that what I lacked in experience of running a business, I would more than make up for with my passion, enthusiasm, and commitment. I would just work out the details as I went along...

One month after that first shoot with my friends, in October 2011, I was visiting my little sister Rosie in Perth, Western Australia. Like us, she had also done the Aussie working holiday thing! I did some serious brainstorming in my notebook on that beach and created 'The Shotgun & Chelsea Bun Club'. I got back from my month in Australia, laid the groundwork, got started and I'd hosted our first 'proper' event with total strangers paying to be there in March 2012. And now you know the rest and everything in between! I remember being absolutely terrified at that first event. I had no idea what I was doing, I was so nervous I could barely get my words out, but I did it and that was the start.

I was so enthused about creating the S&CBC. I remember it being a really exciting time and, in January 2012, I married Keiran. I was so full of love, excitement and possibilities and I was dead set on the intention of being a self-employed married woman!

When we got back from our honeymoon, I went back to work. I knew that I needed to get the S&CBC out there, do more events and make it a viable business so I could leave my job. That's what I did. From January 2012 – June 2012 I carried on with my super early mornings working on the S&CBC and my blog, alongside my day job, and I got it off the ground.

On 4th June, 2012, with no savings, no experience and a hefty car finance payment looming, I threw caution to the wind and quit my day job. I completed my last day at the office and I walked out of the office determined, enthusiastic and with a spring in my step – ready to make my mark on the world!

I soon got into the swing of self-employment and I threw myself into building the S&CBC, doing all I could to grow the business and pay my bills. I had this feeling that I could do anything in business and I was fearless, which served me well to begin with but, because I didn't put the foundations in place, at the end of 2012 I was exhausted.

Fast forward to 2019, with my struggle way behind me, I still have that enthusiasm and passion, but my life is entirely different and I feel balanced and organised.

Five things I have learnt about the journey:

- Even when you are not sure what you are doing or where you are heading, always keep an open mind and keep moving forward. Keep space for unplanned opportunities, because you never know what opportunities will present themselves.
- Special moments really are what life is all about. Create, enjoy and cherish them. It doesn't have to be something grand; a cup of tea with loved ones is as special as anything.
- The best things often happen by accident.
- Sometimes you must give things space for your path to unfold.
- Get out of your own way. Drop the excuses and stories you tell yourself around why you can't do something.

Chapter 3

You Don't Have To Hit Rock Bottom
To Change Your Life

Now we're on to the part where things started to change for me and I took the first steps towards getting my act together and getting balanced. For the first time in a long time, I could start to see a glimmer of hope when it came to a different way of doing things. Enough was enough and I was ready to change my ways.

The catalyst for change came in the form of total burnout. It was pretty grim. For about the tenth time since I had started my business, I had reached the point of total and utter burnout. If you've never had burnout before, then you are lucky. The only way I can describe it is by having all your energy drained, then being flooded with major fatigue and emotional and physical numbness. Burnout totally floors you. It makes you feel detached, devoid of any energy and enthusiasm and it makes you so exhausted that even after twelve hours' sleep, you are still tired.

I had my final big burnout in February 2016. On the third day of ailing and not moving from the sofa, I knew I had to change. Keiran was so good and really looked after me and I felt so loved and supported, even though I felt like a total failure. From that day on, I just decided enough was enough with working myself into the ground. The way I had been doing things was just ridiculous, in fact it was needless. I could finally see it.

At the time, I felt like I just couldn't go on and I remember my mind being all foggy and my body feeling weak, but I kept getting thoughts of change. I had a series of nagging feelings which wouldn't go away, it was like I was mulling through my options. I remember vividly thinking about closing down the club and getting a job – seriously this is how emotionally broken I was! Of course, there is no way I would have done it, but at the time I was so fragile it seemed like a legitimate option. I quickly discounted closure though, too many people needed the S&CBC and I needed it as it was such a big part of me. The only other option was drastic yet positive change, which is exactly what I set out to achieve.

TRUTH BOMB: Even when you think you've got no fight left in you, you can always get up one last time. You can always dig a little deeper

From my propped-up position on the sofa, complete with blanket and vitamin drink, I knew I was really serious about change. I lay there for a while with my thoughts and I remember starting to ruminate over things feeling different and mentally asking myself some 'what if' questions. I was starting to daydream about a different way of doing things; a way that was sustainable and didn't result in burnout. I could feel a spark of hope. As the day went on, that spark grew and turned into a small but fragile flame.

That flame was hope and it was slowly turning into belief; belief that there was another way. This was the first time I could see it.

TRUTHBOMB: Hope and belief can get us through the toughest times

That evening, I took out one of my notebooks and a pen and I started to write down the 'what if' questions I'd been brainstorming. What if I could just work eight hours a day? What if I could sort out all my long-winded processes and save time? What if I could automate a large portion of my business? What if I could outsource admin and social media?

This last episode of burnout taught me a lesson. It made me realise that no matter how dreadful things are, or whatever corner you are backed into, there is always a way out. There will be times when we just can't see it, just as I couldn't see another way apart from all the "busy". Believe me, there is always another way. It took me pushing myself to the point of exhaustion to see this. My hope is that you can believe this and hopefully sidestep burnout, stress or frustration if you are heading that way.

The key thing is that we must be open to find the other way. It might not be obvious and you might have to wait, but another way will always present itself. Things evolve and play out how they are meant to. Sometimes we just need to be patient. I probably didn't expect to change my life at my absolute lowest point, but it evolved that way. So many people want change, but not everyone wants to put the work in. I was ready to change and to find my other way by being willing and putting pen to paper.

I knew I needed clarity, a plan and structure and now I had given myself time and space to work out what that would look like in my notebook.

It started with getting everything out of my head and onto paper. I needed to give myself some mental space to just download everything that I was keeping in my mind that was making me stressed. Just the process of having a mental declutter and getting all of your to-do's onto paper is a powerful and freeing thing to do. Now when I am feeling overloaded, overwhelmed or just a bit out of control, the first thing I do is write it all down.

In my notebook I created a Mind Map of my business with all the different facets and layers. I wrote out headings for each of the business functions: the events, membership, website, admin, marketing and so forth.

Then, under each heading, I wrote all the things that needed doing to have it running in a really slick way – a bit like a step-by-step operations blueprint or manual. This gave me a really clear bird's eye view of what I needed to do to keep my business running within that heading. For instance, with the S&CBC events I wrote out all the things which needed to be done to arrange, book, promote, and execute the events, including all the admin, hosting, preparation and follow up. This really was a fascinating process to go through instead of just having it all in my head!

By listing the operational tasks under each heading, I had such a great overview of what was keeping me busy. Then, I took it a step further and wrote out all the recurring tasks I had to do in my business (this was basically everything I did on a regular basis). After a few hours, I went up a level in detail and organised and identified what my daily, weekly, monthly, and one-off tasks were. I drilled each item down into miniscule detail and realised that I was doing an insane amount of work – no wonder I was exhausted and not performing well.

In 2016, we did 104 ladies' shooting events. I did pretty much all of the admin, organisation, social media and back-office work myself. (Note: I had some amazing members who helped out with emails etc, hosted and really supported me, but admin-wise, it was all on me and that was stressful, in fact it was worse than stressful, it was horriblle).

Once I had my list of tasks, I added a monetary value to each: £5, £50, £500, and £5,000. I added a value to all my tasks and I could see that I was getting bogged down. I was focussing too much on the £5 tasks and not the £5,000 ones! This was really eye opening. I now call this exercise my Clarity Plan, which we will go through in Part Three. My £5 tasks were things like updating the website, replying to tweets, scheduling social media posts, event emails etc. These were low level 'busy' tasks that anyone could do. They didn't directly make me money or further my business in a big way. The £500 and £5,000 tasks were things like creating flagship events, designing merchandise, obtaining sponsorship etc. The higher value tasks were where I should have been focussed, so I could have bought in more revenue, which would have allowed me to get help sooner. Instead I chose to stay down in the weeds with the low value tasks, which I now know is some kind of avoidance and self sabotage!

TRUTH BOMB: Doing what we think is right at the time is enough

After I became really clear as to the detail of where I was in my business, I felt my energy start to come back. Literally it was like a weight lifting off my shoulders and my chest felt a little bit less tight! For the first time in a long time, I felt positive and optimistic. Aside from becoming clear on where I was, it also enabled me to see how far I had come and what I had achieved. That was amazing and I was actually really proud. Even though I hadn't focussed on the big game-changing tasks, I'd still absolutely nailed it!

I carried on writing and next became clear on my goals and longer-term vision. I became serious about what I was trying to achieve. I wrote out three big goals that I wanted to achieve in the next six months. Once I'd defined those goals, I wrote down the action steps I needed to take to achieve them. Just doing this and connecting with what I wanted to achieve, instead of just bumbling through, was huge for me.

This process was game-changing for me as I was able to just mentally offload so much which had weighed me down for so long. By seeing it all in front of me, I knew what I needed to do and I then realised that the answers had been in my head all along – I just needed the time and focus, to be still and to let it all flow.

They say you are born with all the knowledge and experience you need. For the first time in my life I believed it.

I still have the notebook that changed everything. In it is this messy, but amazing bird's eye view of how my business worked. The whole process of putting pen to paper was so liberating and just giving myself the time to do it provided me with fantastic insights.

Once I had clarity on where I was in terms of my newly set goals and vision, it was time to get real with my systems and processes. When I first started out with the S&CBC, I never expected to reach the levels of success that I had. Therefore I didn't ever put the time into establish proper systems.

As my business grew, I hashed together whatever systems I could, but they were never right or enough. I had loads of scrappy spreadsheets, Google Docs and a few website plugins which weren't integrated. I wasn't utilising automation and I had some inefficient processes which kept me busy. I knew I had to identify all these long processes and condense or automate them.

I want to share with you a great example of one of my bad systems and lack of streamlining and automation: my membership onboarding process. I want to illustrate how ill-fitting my systems and processes were. When someone joined as a member, it was such an amazing feeling and I had to go through the steps below to get them enrolled:

1. When a member joins via my website, I receive an email notification (such a great feeling!).

2. I manually added them to a Google Sheet. (There was no database to update or no automation to handle that task for me).

3. Next, I would login to the back-end of my website, confirm their profile and copy and paste their password into a welcome email.

4. I would personalise a welcome email (there was no automation at all) and send it.

5. If the website hadn't captured their home address (often it didn't), I would have to request it via email.

6. Once I received their address, I would update the spreadsheet again.

7. I would hand write a thank you card and send them a badge.

8. Finally, I would add them to the Facebook Group and include them in a welcome post.

The whole process took about ten minutes for each member – no wonder I was worn out! This doesn't sound like a lot, I know, but when they stack up, or when there were variables, it was an awful lot of work. Also, this one simple process was in addition to promoting all the events and keeping everything else going.

I have now managed to remove myself from membership

enrolment with an effective database and membership plugin, which gives me so much time to focus on my members. I had a few similar long-winded processes which needed identifying so I could close the loops, shorten them and spend less time on them, which would enable me to focus on doing meaningful work, not inefficient processes which took me away from my members!

A note here: If you are a brand-new business owner, be sure to start out with sensible systems. You will thank yourself for it in the long run.

It had been so good to start to plan overhauling my systems and to see how I could become more efficient. Once I had done it, I started to think about boundaries. Part of my burnout was caused by always being available to people and always responding. When people wanted something, I delivered, and it wasn't healthy. After some serious soul-searching, I decided it was time to set some proper boundaries. I needed to set expectations with others to get my time back. Simple things, such as autoresponders and proper office hours made all the difference.

After 48 hours and about 50 pages of my notebook later, I was ready. I had gone seriously hard with highlighter pens and scribbles – it was spectacular! Laid out in front of me was my new way, my new life. I had made a switch from being almost defeated, to getting back up and starting over.

The next day, I got dressed and got back to it. My energy had changed entirely and I felt stronger. I knew I had achieved life-changing clarity and that I was on the rise and I was ready to get back to it on my terms, in a structured way.

The first thing I did was find a project management system to organise my notes; a place in which I could create an online action plan for myself. I created an account in Asana. I had used it in the past and it was a fit for my business and it allowed me to create projects, tasks, and to-do's. I added all the past 48 hours' notes and steps over to Asana. It became a logical, sensical, and central management system for my business. I could easily see what was what, add notes and files, and just become organised. (Note this wasn't a database to run my membership from, but rather a system that housed all the day-to-day management of my business).

Asana took away the feeling of overwhelm. It allowed me to see what I had to do and where I was going.

When you are stuck in the middle of the grind / struggle / hustle or whatever you call it, you can't always see things in perspective. When you are drained and busy, it's so easy to overlook even the most obvious of things and it's easy to make mountains out of molehills. I was doing this a lot. Sometimes, we miss the obvious as our focus is elsewhere. My focus had shifted from stress and struggle to possibility, structure, and ease. The more good things I looked for, the more I saw. Something had totally changed in me and I was totally committed to never going back to burnout or my crazy busy old ways.

It is amazing to look back and see how my life changed within the space of about 48 hours; to see how I had gone from total dread and burnout, to hope and clarity. I got back to work and I have not been burnt out since. As time has gone by, my evolution has continued. Over the past few years I have spent a lot of time in becoming efficient, productive and streamlined. Life is way too short to be stuck doing admin that doesn't necessarily need doing.

Once I had entered into this new way of approaching my business, I knew I had to upgrade my whole mindset, too. Even though this positive change had made me feel lighter and more positive, I knew there was a lot more work to do.

In the next chapter I'm going to share with you how the positive momentum built and how £4.99 changed everything.

Chapter 4

The £4.99 That Changed

Everything...

TRUTH BOMB: You always have something to be grateful for

I changed my my mindset and, as a result, my whole life changed.

As the weeks and months went on, I started feeling much stronger and more organised. I was getting into the swing of things with my *"get more streamlined, take the stress off and say no to people more"* approach. I started spending focussed time on a Sunday planning my week in what I call my 'Sunday Session' – something which was new to me, but was actually revolutionary. Giving myself the time to plan my workload increased my productivity tenfold and enhanced my state of mind infinitely. Having a plan meant I started every day knowing what I needed to do. I was taking consistent action towards my goals every day, instead of winging it. I just felt calmer and more capable.

As time went on, there was no Christmas Eve crying, no beds on the sofa, no stress and I actually had proper downtime with my family. I allowed myself to go to my parents without my laptop! Keiran and I started to do normal things, like normal couples. We did things like date night and we went away on holiday and I didn't worry so much about work. I was starting to create a business that didn't need me all the time and that made me feel so good – I was giving myself space to breathe. I was starting to re-evaluate everything and I was making my business run on my terms. I had my passion back to full force!

This is a strange thing to say, but looking back, I was almost glad in a way that I'd had that episode of burnout and how I'd used it for good. I know now that I can find good in almost every bad situation that happens to me. If I can't see good, then I can see the lessons at least.

You know how some things happen in life that aren't pleasant, but, as time goes by, you are glad it happened? That's usually because it allowed something else to slot into place. Remember how you were inconsolable when that guy broke your heart, but you then went on to meet your Prince Charming? That is almost how I feel. If I hadn't had those few dire years of struggle, I wouldn't be writing this book.

My new, more balanced way came exactly at the right time for me. It's funny how things happen which seemingly slot into place.

TRUTH BOMB: Everything happens how it's meant to

Not long after I had my business sorted, I started 2016 strong, clear and optimistic. But I soon quickly got knocked down in that we received the news we had been dreading: My Dad's cancer had spread. He was doing so well and he'd had the all clear from bowel cancer, but now he had secondary cancer in his lungs. It was devastating. None of us saw it coming, not even my Dad and it was a real shock.

I felt as though everything that had happened before, the burnout and the big sort out of my business had brought me to this point for a reason. It was as if I was clearing the decks and working smarter so I could be present with my Dad and family. For the first time, I felt as though the universe had my back and for that I was so grateful.

I was starting to get away from my laptop a bit, eating better and getting out more to do things I wanted to do. I'd gone from working twelve hours a day to about eight hours most days.

In early May 2016, I was in TK Maxx one day, and, as usual, I was lusting over notebooks. Stationery is my vice, I have a mild addiction to it! As I was perusing the stationery aisle, a beautiful mint green A5, leather-bound journal caught my eye. I loved the colour and the gold lettering was just my thing. On picking it up, I saw that it was a gratitude journal. I've always been grateful for a lot, but I'd never really considered journaling or gratitude journaling. I'll be honest, back then it was probably a bit "out there" for me. I bought the book though, because I loved it and thought it would be good to help me get my head around Dad's illness.

It cost £4.99, but brought so much more value. Buying this journal was another one of those moments that would go on to change everything, I just didn't realise that at the time. Little did I know back then, this little journal would go on to change the course of my life.

It took me a few days to get going with my new gratitude journal. It wasn't something I was instantly keen on getting going with. The last time I had kept a diary, it was one of those little ones with a padlock on, when I was about seven. I kept my new journal beside my bed for a few days and, on 12th May 2016, I finally put it to use.

That day we had been to see the consultant with my Dad about his cancer. All of us went en masse to his hospital appointments – it really was safety in numbers, and it was lovely. So we had that horrendous news that the cancer had spread. We were all absolutely devastated. The consultant gave us the news that it would eventually kill him, sooner than we thought.

That night, I went to bed early. I cried for about half an hour. Then, Keiran brought me hot chocolate and I was ready. I wrote my first points of gratitude.

I want to share my actual first entries from my gratitude journal on 12th May 2016:

"Grateful for how nice the consultant was with Dad today and how he was really thorough in answering all our questions."

"For how strong and amazing our precious Daddy is, even with all this going on."

"For Mom being so amazing in caring for Dad; their

devotion to one another is off the scale."
"That Dad got to walk me down the aisle and I'm so grateful for that."
"For my family. We're all so tight, brave and still laugh even when things are this shit."
"That Keiran lit a fire, cooked me dinner and bought me a hot choc."

Being able to look back on that made me feel so good. Right now, it's hard to explain how I felt writing that and reading it back. But I know this is where it all changed. Something changed within me when I was writing those points. If you have a daily gratitude practice, then you will know what I mean. I was looking for the good and it felt really comforting deep in my heart. It felt like therapy. I was absolutely devastated, but I knew I had so much to be grateful for.

TRUTH BOMB: Our lives change through a series of small, but significant moments which all add up

As the weeks and months went on, my personal life was changing in the most heartbreaking way. It felt so great to just be still and to see that I actually had so much going on to appreciate and to be grateful for. It wasn't over with my Dad. Yes, it was horrific to think he was going to die, but he was still here and that was a gift. To be able to see things from that perspective was a gift, too.

I enjoyed that first gratitude entry so much that I carried on with it and wrote in it every night without fail. I did five points a night to begin with. Then, after about a month, I went on to ten things I was grateful for. This little book was changing my life and gratitude was becoming a habit.

Maxwell Maltz, author of the original self-help book *Psycho-Cybernetics*, stated: *"...these, and many other commonly observed phenomena tend to show that it requires a minimum of about 21 days for an old mental image to dissolve and a new one to jell."*

My focus had been on busy for so long, it was as if I had found something that had started to move my gaze up higher.

After a few weeks, I began looking forward to this sacred and special 'me time' every night. I would sit in bed with my bedside lamp on and have ten minutes to recount the day in my gratitude journal. I would reflect on the precious moments I'd had throughout the day and it felt good.

In late May 2016, I started turning my phone off before I got into bed. Revolutionary! I stopped my random late night scrolling through social media and I focussed on myself and all of the good.

Full disclosure: Turning my phone off was a bit of an ongoing tussle to begin with. I would do well for a few weeks, then slip back into late night scrolling again. I didn't beat myself up, though, as I knew that leeway is an important part of achieving balance; being too rigid, is not.

Aside from my gratitude journal, I started to look for the good things in every day. When you start looking for good things, you see more. It is the Law of Attraction (what you focus on expands) and it is part of our physiology.

We all have a small but mighty part of our brain called the Reticular Activating System, or RAS for short. It is a cluster of nerves at the bottom of our brainstem, which is effectively a filter in our brains for our five senses. Our RAS prevents us from being totally bombarded with information. Did you know we are subject to some two million bits of information per second? I can't even begin to comprehend what this even looks like. Our RAS filters out what we want to see and brings it to the forefront of our mind. It serves us up somewhere in the region of 12,000 bits per second. So, if we are positive, we receive more things which make us positive. Likewise, in my struggle, I focussed on struggle, so that is what my RAS served me up.

TRUTH BOMB: What you focus on, you attract. Keep your thoughts positive

We train our RAS to give us what we want in our consciousness. For instance, have you noticed how those who know what they want seem to surge towards it at speed? It's because their RAS is showing them the way and bringing things to help them achieve, based on what it is they want.

Similarly it works with bringing you more of what you are focussed on. You know those people who are surrounded by drama always seem to attract negativity and drama? It's because they are focussed on drama! Likewise with those really jolly people who are always happy, it's because they focus on happy. Or, for instance, if you are looking to buy a new car, then you will probably keep seeing that specific type of car while you are driving. It is no coincidence; your brain is actively looking for it. What you focus on, you attract.

Tony Robbins summed it up brilliantly when he said, *"There's a part of your brain called the RAS and it determines what you notice in the world. When you set a goal, become extraordinarily clear on it, and have strong enough reasons behind your intent, you trigger the RAS. Your brain then becomes incredibly acute at noticing anything that comes into your world that could help you move forward."*

So, why have I brought this up? Because through constantly looking for the good, we can change our reality and our day-to-day life experience. With my daily gratitude journaling, I strengthened my RAS and I created a new habit, a gratitude or a happiness habit. Now I knew this, I knew where I was going wrong.

TRUTH BOMB: Not all habits are bad

I had started to re-programme my mind to bring me things to be grateful for. Summer 2016 felt really good! Keiran and I bought our first house and we were so excited. Rosie and I took our Dad to Germany for cancer treatment with the money we raised by crowdfunding. We were on top of the world. People's kindness and generosity had allowed us two precious weeks in a beautiful clinic with our Dad. When my Dad wasn't having treatment, we'd be out exploring little ski villages hidden away in the mountains. We laughed, ate obscure food, took about a million photos and we were so grateful to have that special, happy time with our Dad.

This all strengthened my RAS. I had an amazing foundation for my new life and I just felt a lot more capable. We had some success in Germany with my Dad and his cancer markers dropped. We were delighted!

I had started to take care of my body, too, and really started to put self-care front and centre. I quit energy drinks and cereal bars, I cut down on my working hours and started going to the gym more. I was doing what was right for me. Would I have done that if I had not developed gratitude? Probably not...

Chapter 5

Supercharging Gratitude And
Knowing Everything Works Out
In The End

As summer turned into autumn, I kept going with my gratitude list every single day. I had cottoned on to the power of peace and quiet and the benefits it brings. I have no idea why I didn't appreciate it years ago..

I looked forward to having some focussed 'me time' every single night. It honestly changed everything for me. I became more selective with this time, turned my phone off more and just shut out the world. It felt amazing!

As I continued to approach things from a place of gratitude, I really felt a shift in my life. I started to feel present and to create a world around me that just felt more relaxed and more intentional. I no longer felt manic or as if I don't have enough hours in the day. I felt in control, because I was in control. I had taken back control.

With my new house and the great summer I'd had with the Germany trip, I definitely felt different. I really felt as if I had this new radiance about me. I felt as though I was starting to really reap the benefits of this smarter way of working and just slowing down. I had this new appreciation about me.

By autumn 2016 we were really settling into our new house and it had really become our home; we absolutely loved it (and still do). We bought a converted Victorian school with double height ceilings and beams. It has so much character and space and it makes us feel so good just being there. You know when a house has a got a nice vibe to it? This is how I feel about ours and it compounded this more positive mindset that I was adopting.

Then, in December 2016, the doctors dropped the bombshell that my Dad's cancer had spread again. We'd been here before but, this time, we were out of options as treatment wouldn't help and his life expectancy was down to two years maximum.

All this appreciation had come at the right time. Everything that I had done with my burnout, my streamlining, my gratitude – it had all got me to this point and I wasn't going to stop.

I started to appreciate so much – all the little things, situations, experiences and feelings that I had never really appreciated before. I felt as though I was magnetising things which made me feel good or grateful. I didn't need major things to make me feel good either. Don't get me wrong: it wasn't as if I was wearing full-on rose-tinted glasses – I just appreciated all the little things. I appreciated sunny mornings, a full tank of petrol, my Dad having a good day, my Mom being chipper, lovely emails from my members and so on.

I felt calmer and more in control than I can ever remember feeling in the past. My friends commented on how chilled I was and that I had changed in a good way. I really felt it too. People commented about how well I looked. I lost weight. I felt authentic, genuine and, for the first time in ages, I was coming from a great place and I wasn't stressed like I used to be. Life wasn't perfect around that time, far from it, but I felt so much better equipped to handle it. I took things in my stride.

With this new mindset track I was on, it really made me honour myself and do more of what was right for me. This included saying no to things. I had given myself the power to say no to obligations and to surrender to what I couldn't control. It was so liberating. All along, I just needed to change my focus and give myself permission.

TRUTH BOMB: Whatever life throws, we handle

So, back to my journal. After about three months, I started doing my gratitude journal in the morning too. This became my Morning Routine. I'd get up 15 minutes earlier and just appreciate the peace and quiet in my house. I must admit, in the middle of winter, it was a real struggle to prise myself out of bed in the cold, but I did it though, every morning, without fail. There were nights when I would be out until late and would have an early start the next day, or even when I'd been out partying, but I still did it. I could have found a million excuses not to do it, but I committed and never skipped a day. By being consistent I was getting results.

The idea of a Morning Routine was to set my day up right. To start my day in the best possible way and to enable me to set my day up for success. Here's what I did:

I would always start the day with a short meditation and just a total quietening down of any negative chatter or racing thoughts. Starting the day with total peace and a quiet mind is one of the kindest things you can do for yourself. Once I had quietened my mind, I would spend a few minutes visualising my goals in minute detail.

In the front of my journal, I wrote down the three big goals I was going to achieve over the next three to six months. I made the commitment to look at my goal list every day and imagine them done.

Every morning, I wrote out my 'Intentions' for the day in my journal. My Intentions were tasks to do, which would help me move closer to my big goals. I also wrote non-negotiable self-care goals. These included things like going for a walk, having a green smoothie, reading my book and other things that made me feel good. These were reminders to look after myself. Self-care was so new to me, so I needed to remind myself to do it.

At the end of the day, I write out my 'Achievements' of that day. The idea was that I would rewrite out my Intentions in the achievements part. It feels so satisfying and it's really good to track my progress and see how far I can go.

Once I had done my Intentions or Achievements, I would write my ten or so points of gratitude and take some time to really feel them. Next, I write a few positive affirmations, then I journal. Sometimes, I journal things which are on my mind or about blocks or worries. Sometimes, it is more of a diary to look back on. At other times, it's a tool for rationalising situations that arise.

One of my huge goals for 2017 was to overhaul the S&CBC membership. I decided I was going to completely rebrand and split my membership off the S&CBC, making it a stand-alone member-ship called 'The Ladies Shooting Club'. It was to be less pink, more grown-up and content- and community-based.

There were a few reasons why I did this massive overhaul. One of the main reasons was that I felt the S&CBC membership needed re-invigorating. There were two main perks at the time for mem-bers: a £10 discount on my events and a members-only Facebook Group.

In parts of the country where we didn't have events, or where members weren't on Facebook, there were no benefits for people to become members. I always felt that I had more to offer and I wanted to create a membership that served more and helped my members up their knowledge and their confidence, and to get out there and enjoy clay shooting as much as possible.

I was so excited about this idea and the prospect of pivoting my business and how it would benefit my members. Creative thinking, start-ups and new projects are my favourite. The new membership is pretty epic and would go on to feature monthly members-only training videos, a success path and an app! I started surveying, brainstorming and planning, I was in my element. My Dad really loved the idea and kindly loaned me the money to have an amazing website and brand built.

I was so excited about the new membership, but you would not believe the amount of blocks I had about it! I experienced so much self-doubt around creating video content and interviewing people. So much self-doubt. Video was so new to me and there was a lot of room for error. All the insecurities came up. *"What if people don't get it?"*, *"What if I talk too fast and look weird?"*, *"What if my members hate it?", "What if I'm really boring?", "What if people say no to me interviewing them?".* I had all the blocks, seriously.

I knew my blocks weren't based in fact; they were just irrational fears. I made a commitment when I was setting up the Ladies Shooting Club to make my dreams bigger than my fears. It really tested my resolve though and the amount of times I nearly quit before I'd even got started was ridiculous. This wasn't like usual self-doubt though, because I had mental space to deal with it.

Because I had created my daily routine, it was like I had the bandwidth and space to get through every single block. I knew I'd tackle them in an empowered way. The old me would have jacked it in under the premise that it was too difficult.

In my daily journal, I added tasks to my daily intention list which would help me get through my blocks. Things like:

- Practice speaking on camera.
- Analyse footage to see if I need to be more / less animated.
- Write scripts so I don't waffle.

I faced my blocks head-on and knew I would make a success of it. There was no way I was going to give into them or give up. I made a commitment to myself and my members. It was an interesting process to go through and to pick them apart. I had never really thought about blocks before. I had always just thought of something as easy, do-able, or hard, which led to me either doing or not doing something.

Now I was facing my fears, pushing the boundaries of my comfort zone and feeling grateful for doing so. I was learning so many lessons and more about myself and resolve. I started celebrating my micro achievements, instead of just forging on to the next task. Things like recording five videos in a day – which was a massive deal to me as I felt so cringey at times and was worthy of a mention in the 'Achievements' section of my journal. I acknowledged myself for these strides forward and it spurred me on more. It felt really good. When I was in my struggle I never celebrated or acknowledged my achievements, I just struggled on. I was finding that by celebrating my achievements, I was feeling good, I was growing in confidence and I was feeling like I could achieve bigger things.

To get through my blocks, I would focus my positive affirmations around how capable I was and how much my members loved the new membership. Then I would write out my fears in my journal section. Most of the *'fears'* lacked substance and, like many of the lies we tell ourselves, there was no proof or truth in them. I broke through every single block and launched the membership. Of course, it was great. The videos were good and none of my fears came true. In fact, I receive regular emails from ladies thanking me for how much some of the videos have helped them. It's funny isn't it! Looking back, I don't see it as a waste of time and energy (my blocks), it was all part of the process.

TRUTH BOMB: Half of the things we fear, never actually happen

All this mindset work I was doing helped me beyond measure in my personal life, too. Without doubt, I would not have been able to handle my Dad's illness as well as I did with my old mindset.

We had some real lows with my Dad. I'm talking full on, *"He's dying!"* and panic-fuelled, *"My parents live in the middle of nowhere! It's going to take 25 minutes for an ambulance to get here"* kind of lows. Or, *"He's in intensive care, his pulse is 20 bpm and he doesn't want to be resuscitated"* – those kind of lows.

In June 2017, I was at my Dad's bedside in Intensive Care, three days before our National Ladies' Shooting Day – my flagship shooting event. Seeing my Dad in that place is one of the most heart-wrenching things I've ever seen. I can't even try to put into words how it feels to see your Dad sedated, having a machine breathe for him and not knowing if you'll still have a Dad at the end of the day. Seeing his chest rise and fall in a mechanical way, the tubes down his throat, the wires all over him, the machines around him bleeping – it was full on.

It was a place we had been before, though – perhaps not to this scale, but we'd had so many dire lows. This time was different, as I decided to look for the good. It was so hard not to focus on the pain of seeing my Dad suffer and you honestly wouldn't have kept an animal alive in the amount of pain he experienced. But I was looking for the moments which were to be celebrated. Fresh coffee instead of tepid tea from the machine. Moments when he came around and smiled at us when he saw us, before the drugs took him back under. Taking a minute to appreciate the strength my family and I had mustered – I was proud of us. Appreciating just what an amazing family I had and how not everyone has that. Appreciating that he was still alive and a part of our lives still.

During times of hardship or suffering, we can always find some good when we look for it. I have also learnt that perspective is a very powerful thing. I know that so many of the things I used to worry about just don't matter and this is such an important message that I want you to understand.

People running you down behind your back hurts, but it's not the end of the world. Your competitor being ahead of you or launching a brand-new product is annoying, but it doesn't take anything away from you.

My message is that we need to take time to stop. We need to keep looking for the good, even when we feel like we are all out of options. I know this sounds easier said than done. It's all about little-by-little, step-by-step, day-by-day, and honouring yourself. When you have the right mindset, you can get through anything. When you change your mindset, your life can change too. Challenges, big goals, major life changes, break-ups, anything: you can get through it all.

My morning and evening routine and all the things I did strengthened my outlook immeasurably. It strengthened my character and it kept me aligned with my goals, my purpose, and it just gave me that confidence that I can do anything.

Here's what my daily practice has evolved into:

- Quiet time to just 'be' and to get me in the best possible mental space. Plus, some visualisation.
- Setting my intentions in the morning and listing my achievements to reflect on at night.
- Writing ten things I'm grateful for, both morning and night.
- Affirmations and journaling or writing.

When we commit to anything new, there will always be resistance. We will be too busy, too tired, too distracted. We give ourselves a hundred different reasons why we can't find the time to commit to something. We must though, as the results can change our lives. We have to be consistent because, when we make consistent action, we get change.

When we do these things on a consistent basis, we form positive new habits. Consistency brings us confidence and through journaling we can get through most things. I am living proof of how you can flip your life when you start a daily practice. Know you can achieve absolutely anything and you will. Since I have been committing to my daily routine, I feel as though I can take on the world. I am not afraid to say no to people if it's not what I want.

I want all of this for you.

If you shift your mindset, you will shift your life – there is no doubt about it. If you invest fifteen to thirty minutes in yourself every morning, things will start to change. Imagine where you will be six months or a year from now. Subtle shifts add up and will become more prominent and other people will notice too.

Chapter 6

Knowing You Can Overcome Anything

TRUTH BOMB: Your life changes when you know you can overcome anything. You make decisions from a place of confidence instead of fear

On 30th October 2017, my whole world stopped and then it changed forever in the most devastating way. My incredible one-in-a-million Dad and my hero, Karl Heinz Lacks, died.

As you can imagine, it was the most unimaginable and, of course, the most utterly devastating day of my entire life.

What I didn't expect though was that 30th October 2017 would be a day that would lead to hugely positive change and lessons: change and lessons that brought me to sharing all this with you. Living through that day, and in fact, the course of my Dad's entire illness, empowered me and made me realise I can overcome anything. This knowledge put me on a totally different path – a path that led to courage, purpose and understanding.

Before he died, I couldn't ever imagine life without him. I cherished every single moment we had together and I felt like we really made the most of the limited time we had. When he was alive, I'd often lie in bed wondering how I'd live without speaking to him every day. I could never imagine not hearing his voice, or laughing at his hilarious laugh, or not watching back-to-back property programmes with him. I couldn't imagine not hearing him saying how proud he was of me or that he loved me again.

Being honest, when he died, I expected that I would fall apart and plunge the depths. I could not envision what getting back up would look like at all. I don't know what I expected my life to be like without him. I just couldn't see it and I didn't want to see it, as he was everything to me.

My Dad worked so hard for us growing up. I felt like I owed it to him to not lead a mediocre life. Strange, isn't it? Maybe I was always destined to rise more when he'd gone? I always promised him I wouldn't let everything fall apart when he died, as he knew how hard I'd worked with the S&CBC to get it to where it was. Like all Dads, he wanted his girls to be happy, healthy and successful. I promised him I would hold it all down and do what makes me happy. I promised him I would always do my best and that is exactly what I am doing.

Looking back, this is the most incredible motivation. Promising your parents you will step into the potential they always hoped for you, is huge.

What I didn't know back then, was how I would go on to use my grief as motivation for leading a better life. I didn't realise that I would really use that motivation and start to step into the potential that my Mum and Dad always hoped for me. I didn't realise that turning my grief around would not only help me, but it's helped others too.

Losing my Dad was hands-down the most devastating and toughest thing I have ever had to go through. It's not as though the sadness ends either. Grief is ongoing. They say grief is pure love and that it takes a year to heal for every year you knew the person.

I agree with this, but I would say that while grief is ongoing, it does change. As I write this, it's nearly eighteen months since he died. There are times when I honestly can't believe he's gone and I full-on burst into tears and I can feel my heart break all over again. Then, there are other times when I feel like I'm coming to terms with it and know I have the best guardian angel ever. I'm not sure I will ever get over losing him, but I know the pain evolves. I am so grateful to have had such an incredible man as my father for thirty-four precious years and for all the lessons I have learnt.

TRUTH BOMB: Things don't happen to you, they happen for you. (Read that again and think about it)

As the months passed following my Dad's death, I set about finding my new 'normal'. Grief has changed me, but not in the way I expected. It made me stronger, clearer and I felt like I had this raw strength to me. It felt like a gift.

Grief made me totally get real about what was important to me and what made me happy. To me, the purpose of life is to be happy and it's how I choose to live my life now, with happiness, in whatever form that is, front and centre. Because if we can't be happy, then, really what is the point of anything? Happiness in whatever form that is: love, experiences, opportunities, people, animals, possessions, whatever. When you are not happy in a situation, you should always look to change it and if you can't change it, change how you look at it.

Losing my Dad made me weigh up everything and pushed me to want to live my best life. I now know first-hand that life is too precious and too short not to live a life I love. It's a strange thing to say I know. This might sound like a cliche to you, but when you realise and believe this, everything changes and you actively live more. You care less what people think and you start to step into your power.

I took my grief and used it to feel empowered, instead of victimised. I took my grief and used it as a catalyst for positive change.

Again, it was like everything that had happened had brought me to this point now. The struggle, the burnout, the gratitude, my Dad's death – it was all a journey. It felt like it was all meant to be, all of it. Now it was this massive, positive change. It was the knowing – the knowing I could now get through anything. My worst nightmare I could possibly imagine had come true in my Dad dying and here I was on the other side, not only surviving, but thriving.

So how do I get through almost anything? For me, it all comes down to approach and mindset. It's about keeping your focus right, focussing on what is more important to you based on what you need to overcome. With my Dad dying it was more important for me to lead a happy and full life, than to fall apart, so that's what I did. It came from putting everything into perspective and sorting out what mattered from what didn't. It was choosing my best life over stalling for the rest of my life with unrealised hopes and dreams. To me, getting through anything has come in the form of perspective, motivation, digging deep and just keeping my thoughts positive. Believe you can and you are halfway there.

To get through anything you have to honour your feelings and heal as much as you can too. You have got to cry when you need to. Don't hold back and treat yourself with compassion. This isn't just about grief, whatever you are going through, be kind to yourself. You can't get through anything if you are worn out, burnt out, or hurting. It's important to allow yourself the time, space and love to heal whatever needs healing. Chances are if you don't deal with or heal what it is, it will always be looming over or eating away at you.

I had a massive emotional clear out of my life not long after my Dad died. It felt amazing and it allowed me to be me. I removed myself from situations. I started saying no to more. I really reduced my obligations and contact with those who put them on me. I retreated to those who I loved the most and I felt so much better for it. I also stopped feeling bad when other people tried to project their insecurities on me. I respected my time more and, as a result, other people did too. When you do something like this, you learn and you become braver.

It is small acts of braveness and pushing our comfort zones that stack up to create big change – the kind of change I experienced. I did little things that pushed and scared me, but I felt better after each one. This mental space gave me more confidence in myself. This confidence, teamed with having more space to be more grateful and to see another way, gave me the courage to go forward. I felt as though I could overcome anything. It is a very special feeling to experience.

I want to take you back to when I was in my struggle. Back then, I had such a closed mindset and it was holding me back. I felt that there was so much I couldn't do. If you can relate to my struggle then hopefully, now you'll see anything is possible.

I could never close my laptop – ever. I couldn't go on holiday without taking a list of work-related items to do with me – ask my husband. I couldn't ever relax – ask anyone who knew me. I could never quit sugar – no way. I couldn't let up, otherwise I'd fall behind – blah.

There was so much I'd tell myself that I couldn't do. However, I had no evidence that I couldn't do any of it. I'd just always assumed that I couldn't, based on my perceived level of discomfort.

Often, it is so much easier to give up and that is what I did so often. I didn't know about the power in pushing through back then. That was where I had got things wrong, I 'thought' I couldn't do so many things, when all along, I could. I had just never committed to trying. This all seems so trivial to me now, but back then, it was a problem.

TRUTH BOMB: You really can get through anything when you believe it. Do what you can to affirm belief

I now know I could do all this and a lot more – I now know I can do anything.

In the same vein, I hadn't really ever tried to confront my fears head-on to find their underlying cause. We all have rational and irrational fears. To me, my Dad dying was a rational fear. I had a fear of public speaking and I had a fear of being in a lift for more than five seconds if it didn't move!

Irrational fears were things like members cancelling en masse, someone giving the S&CBC a bad review, a host not turning up… These fears are usually based in insecurities and never actually happen!

Changing your motivation or the meaning of what it is you are worried about is one way to deal with fear. What's more important to you: making your dreams a reality, or not achieving them because you are so loyal to your inner voice and ego?

Some of us just have the fear and we accept it. We tell ourselves things like, *"Oh yeah, I just can't do that,"* or, *"I'm so rubbish, I'll never be able to do that,"* and they don't ever try. These people likely won't ever change. They can change – they can do anything, but they are usually too frozen with years of limiting beliefs.

How about on the flipside: Quite often, it is not the fear of failure that we're scared of, but the fear of success. With success comes change, and some people fear change. This sounds crazy to some people, but does it resonate with you? If you fail at something, you get back up and try again, or you can revert to your comfort zone for a while. Failure is the norm for a lot of people. If you succeed in a big way, things will likely change for you, people might treat you differently, you might have to step up to be that person you might not be ready to be.

How amazing, though? How amazing to be so successful and to grow so much as a person?

When you feel strong and in control, that's when you can overcome anything. That, or when you are forced to overcome things. When push comes to shove, you tap into the amazing reserves of resilience we all have.

I overcame most things because I changed my mind and because I told myself I could. Telling myself this led to a feeling, which led to making it happen. Action creates momentum – positive or negative.

I want to give you an example of how I overcame two different and difficult situations at either ends of the scale: One fear based in business, one mindset based in life. No matter how big or small, we can get through most things.

I had a fear about writing this book! The irrational fear was I was taking a massive risk and it could backfire in a big way. This was because my business and passion is shooting and I'm well known in that industry and have an audience of people who expect that from me. The thing is, I'm writing this book about my journey, mindset and how to make your business balanced, so I have people who will no doubt judge me and to me it just felt like a risk.

There were a few times when my subconscious would start with the usual dialogue of trying to talk me out of it: *"Who are you to think you can write a book?", "Who's even going to care?!", "You are embarrassing yourself*". I heard it, but I knew I would over-come it because I know it's irrational. There was no evidence, so it was a no-brainer not to listen. I told myself all the reasons I could do it instead. I countered the negative thoughts with things like: "*I've been through my journey for a reason. I've changed my life in the most incredible way and I have a duty to share this with others*". Or "*If you inspire just one person, it's been worth it. To one person you might change their world*". I shifted my focus, pulled back some perspective and I reframed it. It wasn't a major irrational fear, but it did play on my mind a lot. It's only a small block, but it was nearly big enough to derail me, so I knew I needed to overcome it.

My second example is where Keiran and I finally got pregnant in early August 2018. We'd been trying for nearly a year, so you can imagine how ecstatic we were when we found out! It happened in Barbados in August 2018, our favourite place on earth. Our parents were delighted at the prospect of being grandparents. We told a select few people and started discussing car seats and baby names – it was the dream and we couldn't be happier!

One day in October Prince Harry and Meghan Markle announced they were pregnant. The day the world had gone into baby fever; and the day I had a miscarriage.

I was of course delighted for Harry and Meghan, but it felt like a bad joke. That wasn't the hard part though. The hard bit was feeling my body change and grow, then feeling it all shrink and change back was immensely difficult.

Two days later, Keiran and I got home from hospital after my final doctor's appointment and I went to bed about 2pm. I cried and I didn't get up until the next day. I gave myself a week off and just went easy. We were lucky. Things do happen in life that seem so cruel and so pointless, but we can learn from them.

I was able to overcome this quite quickly as I knew I had a lot to be grateful for. Things like that it happened at ten weeks and not thirty weeks or even later. I took the fact that my body does work, so that's a blessing. That I had unbelievable support around me and that I had my little S&CBC dream team keeping things going.

In the coming days and weeks, I journaled around what had

happened. It enabled me to reframe things and to move forward. We don't forget things that shape us or hurt us, but we grow with them, take the lessons and overcome them.

It is important to feel that sadness but, when you are ready, you need to move on and cut things loose. Tragic things happen to us, but we always grow through and come out stronger, no matter how long it takes. It's about brushing ourselves off and getting back up again.

We can plan for most things, but there will always be obstacles and challenges that will crop up and push us to new levels. It's not a disaster if you make mistakes, because you learn from them and mistakes are proof you are trying. Think back to my Christmas Eve near bankruptcy – it wasn't a disaster as I didn't let it become one.

Whether it's grief, a breakup, losing a job, being on the brink financially or something else. When you walk the path, eventually there comes this quiet strength and courage. No matter how tough things are for you in any given moment, you adapt, you learn and you evolve. To me keeping the faith is key. The faith and knowing that a month or year from now, you'll be in a totally different place.

Sometimes we will hit rock bottom and that's ok. From rock bottom we can rebuild and start again.

Even if you don't have a clear path, you have always got options and you must take that first step to get going. This is the path that becomes apparent as you start walking. It won't be straight and well-lit, but it does get you on the road. There are times when I've not wanted to walk that path. I've had to drag myself along it on my knees, kicking and screaming, but I did it, and it always got me to a better place. If you have got a path that needs walking and you have been putting it off, just take one step, then another, then another.

Think about what in your life now is really challenging or worrying you, what is really giving you grief and keeping you up at night? What would you have to do to overcome those things? Can you look at them in another way?

Making your dreams bigger than your fears is the key to massive success. Imagine a life or business where we took intentional action, but ignored fears? Imagine how our lives would look?

Chapter 7

There's Always Good

"Sometimes you win, sometimes you learn"
John C Maxwell

I love this quote and often throw it out there when things don't go to plan. It's usually said to gloss over something which didn't go how I expected it to, a perceived failure or some other kind of hash. There is a lot of truth in it though. Sometimes you do win and things go to plan beautifully, other times they just don't. Whatever we try to do, things just don't go to plan. When this happens, we must look to see what we have learnt, then we must try again.

Since coming through my struggle I've been open and learnt a lot of lessons. I like to think of them as my lessons in life as each one of them has been a part of this massive personal growth that I've been going through.

I want to share with you my five top lessons in life based on what I've learnt. I want to remind you that lessons are everywhere. We can even find them in the darkest of places. Like with my Dad, it was so unbelievably sad, but so incredibly transformational at the same time. Life is what you make it and you can make it better every day!

I've talked about it already, but my biggest lesson from the past few years is that there is ALWAYS something to be grateful for.

TRUTH BOMB: Always be learning. Always be looking out for lessons, they are everywhere

Lesson 1) Failure isn't actually a bad thing, nor is it final

I feared failure for so long. When I really look into why that is, I know it was the thought of looking silly and what other people would think, or just not knowing what to do and feeling helpless. Of course, I know now that it's unfounded and it doesn't really matter what people you don't love think and, actually, no one knows everything! There were times when I'd fail and I'd take it to heart and really give myself a hard time. Big or small things, to me a fail was a fail. Then there was labelling myself as a failure. Ugh. How many times have you thought this about yourself? It's so bad, isn't it? What I know now is that you are not failing if you are trying.

I failed my driving test on the first attempt – that stung. I failed some exams – that stung too. I had some failed relationships, which really stung but, from all of them, I learnt something. Particularly not braking too hard, that Geography wasn't my thing and the boyfriend wasn't the one anyway. What I know now is that so-called failure is something we all must go through in order to succeed. It's a part of the growth process and instead of it being avoided at all costs, it is to be applauded. You are taking action and you are trying. You are trying all the ways to get to where you want to go.

If you are trying something which isn't going to plan, that's fine. Stop, re-adjust, figure it out and try something else, a new approach. It's just a lesson and, if it's not going to plan, you are not on the right path. It's teaching you new ways, resilience, patience, innovation and more.

TRUTH BOMB: Trying is not failing. Not trying is failing

Lesson 2) Health is Wealth

Isn't that the truth? Mind, body, and soul. If your health isn't good, then you are limited.

I'm going to use my Dad as an example again, as this really rang true with him. Cancer eventually took away his freedom. Slowly at first: things like not being able to fly on an airplane because of the air in his lungs. Then he couldn't walk far because he couldn't breathe. Then he couldn't walk to the car because he couldn't breathe. Then he couldn't leave the house. Then it was hard for him to leave his bedroom, because he couldn't breathe going up the stairs. Eventually, not for long thankfully, my Dad was a prisoner in his own home.

No amount of money, fast cars or designer clothes would have made any difference to him. What mattered to him were moments. Making the most of moments when people came to visit. Celebrating tiny wins like getting out of bed unattended, making it downstairs for a few hours etc.

When you have your health, *generally* you have your freedom. You have the freedom to try and the freedom to do.

Health is a mindset too – it's about feeling good and it's about self-care. When you take good care of yourself, you are brighter, more capable, more energised. You are more optimistic, positive and you see the way forward easier.

Self-care, I think, needs more of a mention here too. To me, self-care is a very broad topic that means different things to different people. To me, it means rest and recharging. It is about following my heart and doing what feels right for me. It is about putting myself first: making the most of that quiet time before the day picks up pace; having a shower, getting dressed and nourishing myself before I start work; having regular breaks throughout the day; moving and stretching; being outside; having the weekends off; eating and sleeping well, having space around me. Sometimes self-care means booking myself in for a massage, going to the gym or just having a nap in the day. Whatever makes you feel nourished and recharged!

What is your self-care situation like at the moment? Do you even have enough time to rest? Start to think about how you can incorporate more self-care into your life every single day, even if it's just five minutes somewhere. As with everything in this book, it involves small actions, little by little, step by step, day by day.

I want to touch on money vs health. If your business or job is making you ill, then you must change. Just like me with my burnout (I'm going to take you through, step by step, in Part 3 exactly how I changed). I couldn't have gone on the way I was. If I had, I would have ended up doing some long-term damage to my health. When I made changes, my life opened to this journey. Wealth isn't always money – it's freedom, it's choice, it's love and abundance in all those areas.

Lesson 3) Everything always works out in the end

You've just always got to believe it. Life will take us on some real rollercoasters and there will be bizarre twists of fate that are just dire. Situations arise that you think you'll never get out of or will never end. But... I honestly believe they do.

Most situations that we go through are temporary and are usually just one part of many layers of our lives. When things blow up or go wrong, we tend to magnify the situation to take over our whole life. We put our Drama Lens on which we view things through. Sometimes we have just got to surrender to what we can't control and have faith that it will work out.

We've got to just do what we can, not view our whole life through one event and hold on to that faith, even when all else seems lost. We need to keep our eyes open for people coming into our worlds, or opportunities that open up to help us.

We don't always get the outcome we want. Sometimes we get an outcome we could never have imagined possible, but we will always get the lessons. It might take months or even years, but it will definitely work out in the end.

Lesson 4) Your Life is happening now

You are alive in this present moment. Not when you win the lottery, lose the weight, or meet the love of your life. There will be a time in the not too distant future when you look back on this time so fondly and they will be your Golden Years! Maybe in the future you will wish you can rewind to now. Maybe you don't have the worries now you may have in the future. Maybe you won't have some special people around you or the job you have now. Life moves fast. I can't stress how important it is to take notice of what's going on around you.

In my struggle I was always so fixated on the future: when I'd have more time, money, freedom etc. I was always on to the next thing to get some kind of gratification. All I really needed to do was slow down and to take note of all that was going on around me. Thank goodness I know this now.

You've got to make the best of this time. Fix things that can be fixed. Make peace with your past and quit the job you hate. Put your phone away and give your full attention to the people you are with. Focus on the work you are doing to do a good job. Just pause when you are outside and take a moment to enjoy all the beauty around you.

You can't ever get this time back and, just being brutal, tomorrow isn't guaranteed. I know you are busy and I know you are doing your best, but take time to slow down now and then to appreciate all that is around you.

Don't look back a year from now with regrets.

Lesson 5) Don't take things or people for granted

Take people for granted and they become resentful. Sometimes people don't mean to take you for granted, but they do. Always be aware of the people in your life and always be grateful for them. Thank people and let them know you appreciate them. The person I took for granted was my darling Grandma Ivy. She was always there and I just always expected her to be, until one day she wasn't. I never got to ask her all the questions I meant to ask her about the war or growing up. I guess I thought she'd always be there. If you have someone in your life who's always there, just tell them you love them or just acknowledge them. It can mean the world to them. Just like when someone does it to us. It's such a simple act, but it can change everything.

Having a miscarriage taught me a lot too. This was a classic example of not taking anything for granted. You never know what's going to happen tomorrow, so you've got to do what you want now. It taught me patience. It taught me timing and how some things you can't rush and how they just need to happen in their own time. It taught me we must honour our feelings and that life goes on.

Lesson 6) Living your purpose

You've got to go with what feels right; living a life that doesn't feel aligned will ultimately make you resentful and lower your energy levels. In my day job, before I set up the S&CBC, I was rotting away, my soul was dying. I couldn't cope with the mundane and mediocrity. The risk of leaving a salary and the known, to me, far outweighed the risk of having no plan or no money. I had to try and I was prepared to fail. The trying is the crucial part. No one will ever knock you for trying.

There were so many lessons I learned from being brave and jacking in my job. Imagine if I hadn't jumped ship? I would probably be a middle manager at best, in a job with no soul (not that there's anything wrong with that, it's just not me). I would be filled with regret for not mustering up the courage. I would probably hate myself every day for not following my heart, even though I wasn't ready or prepared. Unrealised potential just wasted. My relationships and health would have suffered and I wouldn't be the vibrant woman I am today. When you are unhappy, it affects EVERYTHING. When you live your purpose, you get vibrancy and you get into a state of flow.

My lesson in this isn't that if you take a risk, you will automatically win. My risky leap into self-employment, as you know, wasn't all roses. It's about taking a risk in the direction of your dreams and seeing what happens. There were times during the early years of the S&CBC when I longed for sick pay and just working 35 hours a week, but look at me now. I don't have it all figured out yet and I know I'm nowhere near reaching my full potential, but I am trying, every single day. I'm showing up and I'm trying.

Always be on the look-out for lessons. Don't take things to heart, take the lessons.

Chapter 8

What Balance Is To Me

We know that we can overcome most things when we have the right approach. It's true that there are some situations which we can't turn around, or from which we can't take any good, but we must ensure that we take time to heal from them, whatever they are.

Overcoming tough periods in our lives, or challenges, I believe starts with just believing you can do or get through it. It's having that belief and keeping strong, even when you are not entirely sure that you can do whatever it is you want to do. That is what got me through. It is so unbelievably simple, I think we just all overlook it.

During my struggle, I just didn't know this and my life reflected that. My inner world was chaotic and I reflected that into my outer world and my day-to-day experience. Things were frantic and messy.

In this chapter, I want to share with you what my life is like now and how it has all changed. Then I want to go into more detail on what balance means to me and encourage you to start thinking about what it means to you.

I can't put my finger on exactly where my life swung into what it is now. I can't say for sure if it was the burnout and discovering gratitude which really changed everything, or if that was just the starting block. Losing my Dad obviously really changed everything once and for all, and compounded everything. Maybe I'll never know why it took me so long to get started or to get here, but I know this is a much more comfortable and enjoyable way to live.

TRUTH BOMB: We were born to thrive and not just to survive

I want to share with you to what my life is like right now. Knowing everything I know now, I've been able to make positive changes and do what feels right for me. First up, nothing is perfect and things are always evolving; and I think it's important to remember that. But when we are ready to change and make it happen, we start to take those crucial first steps.

I've been very lucky in that I have managed to structure my days and weeks to suit me. I now live more than I work, which, when I consider my journey, makes me massively proud of myself for getting myself in this position.

Most weekdays, Keiran and I wake up at 6:00am and we take turns to make the coffee, as we're sweet like that. I haven't even mentioned how much my marriage has changed in the most beautiful way since I started this journey. Just know we have never been happier.

Once we've had some coffee, I stretch and then I do my Morning Routine. Often, I start it by lighting a candle and closing my eyes to quieten my mind for ten to fifteen minutes. After that, I'll spend about fifteen minutes with my intentions, gratitude, affirmation and journaling. I really savour these moments in the morning, as it is a time of just absorbing the peace. Setting my day up for success is so important to me. I don't turn my phone on until I've done all that. Then I move, which usually means a walk in the countryside.

Then at around 9:00am, I open my planner and laptop.

When 9:00am comes around, I am grounded and starting my day in the best possible way. That sacred time to myself is so important to me. It ensures that I start the day in a calm and intentional way, and sets the tone which usually continues through the day. I say 'usually' as things occasionally happen that can knock my calm vibe, even with the best intentions.

Each day, I know what I need to do to get me closer to my goals, because I plan my workload for the coming week in my Sunday Session. Everything is right there in my planner, waiting for me. I like to write my goals and intentions for that day in my journal to ensure that I really commit to them. I find this quite empowering and it gives me an extra little bit of clarity.

I factor a bit of time into every day for things that aren't expected but need my attention too. This allows for all those unexpected emails and phone calls. That daily time buffer makes me feel calm, ready and able to take it all on.

Then it's on with my day. I work six hours per day now. It feels so good to clock off at 3pm to do what I want to do! I quite often have to pinch myself, because I am so lucky.

I do some form of exercise every single day; whether it's walking our dog or going to the gym or yoga, I make it happen. During my struggle, I was always slumped over my laptop or in my car and I felt as though I was really stagnating. I now know that I must move every day to keep my energy up and my body and mind in good form.

Movement to me forms part of self-care and self-care leads to balance. It took me a while to achieve an even kilter with self-care. It took me a while to get to a point of ditching the energy drinks in favour of nourishing smoothies and being in bed by 10:00pm, but I am there now. I now know that I can't lead a life I love if I'm not nourished, well rested and clear-headed.

So, as you know, all of this didn't happen overnight and my journey was one of gradual and incremental changes. Drastic change can lead to quitting, so I always advocate steering clear of being drastic. I recommend sustainable and consistent baby steps. It's about edging towards balance instead of jumping to the other side of the see-saw.

Little shifts and doing things consistently will add up to new ways, which in turn become new habits. These habits change our lives and change us physiologically too.

Remember Dr Maxwell Maltz, the author of *Psycho-Cybernetics*? Dr Maltz said, "*It requires a minimum of about 21 days for an old mental image to dissolve and a new one to jell.*" This is all I've done and there's been a ginormous change to my life in a relatively short space of time.

I now have several good habits (there was a time when it was ALL the bad habits!). Gone is the social smoking, worrying, binge eating and other health hazards. Now, my biggest habit is positivity. I have a mantra (in case you hadn't noticed!) of *"little by little, step by step, day by day"*. Staying true to these nine little words took me from burnout to balance.

Allow me to share with you what balance means to me.

Balance, to me, is a combination of so many things. It's give and take; it's ease and lessons; it's freedom and structure, it's love and it's not loving. Balance allowed me to get my life in order. Once I did that, things started to flow.

It's getting my best work done, but it's also having fun. It's me time, family time and it's going overseas. It's all the things I love to do. When we go too far one way, we can't function as we're meant to and, too far the other way, it's unsustainable. Balance is straight down the middle of everything.

The universe is balance. The world is balance and we all need balance to thrive.

Here are a few examples of what balance means to me:

- Living a life with low stress and pressure.
- Having time to do meaningful work and to make an impact.
- Running a business which doesn't run me.
- Having evenings and weekends off, laptop free.
- Having time to properly switch off and unplug.
- Putting myself first and nourishing my mind and body.
- Knowing all I can do is my best.
- Knowing that whatever happens, I can get through it.
- Being ok to not be perfect or have it all figured out.
- Being a good wife and a good leader.
- Having steady energy.

I want to tell you how much I seriously value ease. That means ease in my day (and setting it up right). Ease in my relationships, in my work, in my relationships with the people around me and most importantly, with myself. Ease means losing that anxious feeling in our chests and feeling rushed. It's letting go of what other people think about us (their thoughts and their opinions are on them). It's letting go of what we can't control and it's doing the best we can with what we have. When you have balance, you have ease.

Find out what balance is to you. My kind of balance and harmony might be the total opposite to yours. It's all about finding what is right and what works for you.

What kind of habits do you need to kick and which ones do you need to embrace? Start to think about that.

As an example, like many people, I was totally addicted to my phone. I would be on it all the time, checking work stuff and replying to messages rather than engaging in conversation, and caring more about what strangers on the internet were doing. I'd be on it as soon as I woke up. I'd waste a lot of time throughout the day too and I'd lie in bed scrolling. I knew this had to stop, as it was becoming a problem. I didn't want to be one of those people who was always glued to their phone.

I knew I had to break the habit, so here's what I did:

- I put my phone on silent all the time (if I was working and someone called, it would ring via my laptop so I wouldn't miss it).
- I took email off my phone.
- I use an App called RealizD that tracked the amount of time I spent on my phone.
- I'd do the screen free challenges on the RealizD app a few times a day.
- I don't go on my phone until I've done all I need to do for myself in the morning.
- The biggie: I made our bedroom a phone free zone.

Cracking my phone habit felt so good. I wasn't always worrying about what was going on. It took me about a month to really stick to it. I reduced my social media use to an hour a day and I challenge myself every day to keep it inside that. My life is just better when I focus on myself instead of what everyone else is doing.

That, to me, is balance. Balance isn't comparing yourself to others on Instagram or getting waylaid reading Twitter feuds. Equally, it isn't about feeling like you are missing out.

As I became more focussed, I started to block my time. I noticed I was intentional and productive at the start of my day, from about 9am to 12:30am. Then I'd taper off and slump after lunch. My energy was all over the place.

It occurred to me that I wasn't moving enough. Quite often, I'd do my whole six hours without really moving. So, I started breaking my to-do list down into one-hour blocks. This supercharged my productivity and my energy!

I started setting a timer for an hour on the phone and I'd work on one thing only. Then, once my hour was up, I'd get up and move. Sometimes, I'd get a drink; sometimes I'd get up and let the dog out or even just stretch. I learned that I just needed to move – not for long, but something.

These time blocks were amazing. Not only was I getting a lot more done, because I was having so many little breaks, but I could go all day without tapering off too much energy wise.

With balance comes leeway. You must give yourself leeway or it isn't balance – it's a quest for perfection, but we can't be perfect all the time and we need to remember that. Sometimes, we just need to give ourselves a break. Leeway is being kind to yourself and giving yourself a margin for being human.

A few examples for you about how I have leeway in my life now:

- If something doesn't go according to plan, it's ok, I re-adjust.
- If I must pull an eight- or nine-hour shift in the office, I do, but then I only work a few hours the

following day.

- If I can't go to the gym, I'll go for a walk.
- If something breaks or goes wrong, I fix it the best I can.
- I give other people leeway – so many of us need it.

When we don't have any leeway, we can become resentful of all sorts of things.

Saying no to things with which we don't feel aligned, is balance. This includes anything that affects our mood in a negative way. Feeling obliged isn't nice, so just say no where you can.

You are not a bad person for saying no – you are doing what's right for you and that is most important. You are protecting your energy.

Balance is recreation. We must make time for play and to just chill. As someone who is running a home, family and an empire or maybe a second job, we must have downtime to recharge. If you are 'too busy', find just five minutes here and there to sit down and just breathe. Better still, block out time in your calendar for having fun – the more the better! When you have fun, you are easier going, more creative and far nicer to be around! Time for recreation isn't selfish – it's essential. The better you look after yourself, the better you look after other people, and the better you can show up as the best version of you.

Recreation to me, at the moment, is travel. I never used to allow myself a proper break and now I can't get enough! I was born in the wrong climate, as I thrive in the heat! I go away often these days – sometimes, I take my laptop and it's a working trip, just to go away to get inspired.

Other times it's a holiday and I switch EVERYTHING off. What I really love about going away is having that space and knowing I'll come back the best version of myself. I know I'll come back with tons of inspiration. If you can get away more, I highly recommend it.

I've had life-changing inspiration when I've been laying on a beach! I mean, how could you not be inspired being surrounded by beauty and space?

Just for the record, I don't spend a ton of money on holidays either. Use your network and see what you can do. To me, recreation changes everything as it gives us something positive to focus on and it replenishes our energy. I've said it a million times before, but you can't do your best work when you are stressed or exhausted!

On the flipside of recreation is structure. Structure to me is the framework and the blueprint, and routine is the doing.

I think of structure as more long-term and getting organised so you know what needs to be done. Structure brings discipline, too. When you work from home, you can create structure to the way you get up, get dressed and set out time for certain things.

When you put a structure in place and get into a routine, you give yourself the best possible chance of success and balance. Let's be honest, many of us wing it and flounder daily. I know this, because I used to do that in a big way!

Having structure and routine straightened me up in ways you wouldn't believe. It dialled stress and anxiety right down, because I knew what I was going to do the following days, weeks, months and years to achieve my goals.

Creating structure requires some planning. I loved creating mine as I felt invigorated by the process. Setting routines required clarity and consistency. We will go into all this later.

So, as you know by now, I am testament to having the right mindset. If you get on the gratitude and mindset wagon today, imagine how much change and balance you can achieve in the next month. It might work for you to do it all at once, or it might be more sustainable to start small and add layers as you go, just like I did. Whatever is right for you, do that. Just be consistent every single day and I promise you will achieve the results.

So, what else is balance to me? It's focussing on the good every day. It's doing work in the most efficient way. It's getting fresh air and being outside. It's eating well, but still enjoying a few glasses of fizz, or delicious chocolates when I want to. It's giving myself time to take a breather and step away.

Start to think about what balance means to you. What aspects of your life knock you out of balance?

Start to think about where in your life you go too far the other way. Are you always on your phone and not engaging in real conversations? Would you like to stop always comparing yourself to others? Are you too busy and stressed?

In Part Two, we will look at mindset in a big way and start to take some action!

PART 2
MINDSET

Chapter 9

The Power Of Perspective

"The world changes when we change our perspective"
Unknown.

I didn't really understand the power of perspective as well as I do now before 30th October 2017 – the day my Dad died.

He started the dying process on 28th October. He was at home in his bed, right where he wanted to be. My Mum, sisters, aunts, uncle and our darling 89-year-old Grandma Phyllis (Dad's Mum) were all there by his bedside.

It was the most surreal forty-eight hours of my life. I didn't quite appreciate the entire range of emotions I would feel. There was happiness, relief, laughter, despair, chaos, the most unbelievable sadness, pride, and so much more. It was the whole spectrum.

Those forty-eight hours were beautiful in a surreal way. There was so much love in my parents' house, it was ridiculous. You could really feel the overwhelmingly powerful and loving energy in the bedroom where my Dad was. It was pure love in every possible form, whether it was through tears, laughter, sharing moments, or reliving the good times.

Over that weekend, we crammed so many people into my parents' bedroom. We all took turns to make cups of tea, to sit on the bed next to him and to hold his hand and to just talk to him. All the people that meant the world to him were right there with him. He knew we were there, and none of us left him.

We knew this was the end and there would be no going back.

Strangely, we were all so strong and focussed on the love. I guess we all thought we would be in pieces, but we had this air of love and strength within us.

Strangely, that day, for the first time in my life, I saw a deer at my parents' house. I looked out of their bedroom window and saw a deer grazing quietly below the window. I had never seen a deer there prior to that day, or since..

If you have never seen a person die, it is so hard to explain the process. Their breathing changes and you just know they are never coming back. Their skin goes pallid and the colour of their lips lightens. It is humbling in a way and yet such an absolute privilege to see someone transition and fade away. You just know your life is never going to be the same again but, what you don't appreciate in that moment, is that your life will go on.

It might seem impossible to see, but it's true. You might also become a better version of you, when the sadness evolves and subsides. Just like I did. The thing is you just never know how you are going to react – you just can't predict it.

After nearly two days of solid bedside vigils, the family all started to leave to go and get some sleep. My sister Rosie, Keiran and I finally left on that Monday night about 11pm. Dad passed away in his bed with my Mum holding him about forty-five minutes after we left. Just the two of them. Pure love.

He waited for his girls to go so we didn't have to see him leave. He faded away in my Mum's arms. How beautiful is that? Unbelievable amounts of love, even when taking his last breath.

TRUTH BOMB: Life is not forever, but love is

The course of the next few days were a blur. We all went to my Mum's the next day. The undertaker didn't come until 3pm in the afternoon and we all just sat with him drinking tea as we had done for the days before. Cousins came to say their goodbyes and my grandma, aunty and uncle came back. We were all just one, bounded by love and just wanted to be together in that bubble.

Through the tears, I remember looking at my Dad's lifeless

body and feeling so proud and honoured to have had such an incredible human as my Dad. I tried to imagine what he would have looked like as a grey old man, but here he was, perfectly still and as handsome as ever – perfectly perfect. In that moment, I knew something had changed in me and I was no longer the person I was a few days before.

Reminder: Never underestimate the power of a single moment.

What I didn't know in that moment, was that I was about to step into my power and change my life; courtesy of this precious perspective I'd just been served.

Down under the initial shock and grief, I knew I would no longer waste a moment on things that didn't matter. It was time to take my balance journey a step further and chase my dreams harder. It was time to let go of things that were holding me back or bringing me down.

And there it was, as I sat next to my Dad's body. The question hit me: What was it that really mattered to me?

Did other peoples' deadlines, thoughts, expectations, needs, insecurities, egos and agendas matter? Throughout my Dad's illness, was he thinking, "I *haven't replied to someone's email*," or "*Damn...someone unfriended me on Facebook*"? Was he concerning himself with peoples' opinions, or was he wishing he'd lost a few pounds? No, of course he wasn't! He was focussed on love, family, being present and just 'being'. Nothing else mattered. When I pondered that, it just felt so freeing.

TRUTHBOMB: Great things can happen even in the saddest moments. Stay open to looking for them

Perspective is the most powerful thing we can have, especially when we know how to harness it. Perspective can change everything – it absolutely did for me. I just knew I had to keep it in mind and keep my focus on the question: *"What really, honestly, truly, matters deep down?"*

Perspective makes the things that don't matter fall away. If it doesn't move me forward, make me happy, or align with me, then it doesn't get my focus. Time is too precious to waste on the trivial issues and things we can't control. We must keep perspective.

Back to my Dad. In a strange and roundabout way, I am so fortunate that I went through his illness and death with him. I would, of course, give ANYTHING to have him back and I'm sure you can imagine how many nights I have cried myself to sleep, or how many times I have had pangs of sheer panic that hit me that he's not here. Going through his brave and courageous journey, he showed me that there is always good in everything. I talked about this with him when he was in hospital, but I took this with me when he died.

There is always good. You just have to look for it. I could see so much good as I sat next to my Dad's body. Good is always there.

I took a few weeks off after losing my Dad. I wanted to be with my Mum and sisters. We all needed time to process what had happened and just to recover. My best friends rallied round, kept my business running. People I hadn't spoken to for years reached out and even strangers got in touch to wish us well. It was humbling and so important to have that space to process what had happened and to start healing.

I honestly believe perspective is a gift. When we use it positively to look at something, we change our view, our beliefs, our actions, our outcomes, and ultimately our lives.

You might not have had a life-altering event yet and it doesn't take one for everyone to get some perspective – sometimes you just need to get really honest and real with yourself. Start to think about perspective and what really matters to you at a soul level. I am not talking material 'things' or people-pleasing here. I am talking full on, deep-down, what really matters to you.

I could have quite easily let everything go business-wise during 2016 and most of 2017. 2018 had its challenges with grief as well. The first anniversary of Dad's death and getting his headstone installed was awful. If you have lost a parent or someone close, you will know how utterly heartbreaking it is to see your loved one's name etched in stone, with the dates they were born and died on.

As you know, not long after my Dad died, in Spring 2018 I lost my beautiful grandma, Ivy. She was always there for us when we were growing up and at every major life event and moment. We all loved her so much. She had the most hilarious sense of humour and in fact, she died on April Fool's Day, which was like a last joke from her! She flirted with any man who dared speak to her and she had the heart of a lion. God forbid anyone who upset my Mum or sisters. Grandma Ivy was fiercely protective, loving, loyal and one of the most generous people I knew.

Four months later, in August 2018, one of my best friends, Pip Watson died; another person who was so loved, lost to cancer. Pip was a real rock for me in 2016 and 2017 during my Dad's illness and death. She was instrumental in the growth and success of the S&CBC. Again, she was such a strong, straight down the line and brave woman. A few weeks before she died, she was shooting at a S&CBC event with us. Her strength and character were incredible. I would have probably folded the S&CBC and never started the Ladies Shooting Club (and likely never started this book) if Pip hadn't appeared in my life. I owe her so much.

Three people who I loved to the moon and back had died in the space of nine months and, eight weeks after losing Pip, we had our miscarriage. But, because of my new approach, I was able to get through it all by focussing on my new-found perspective. I was able to feel all the love and look for the best in what was the most unimaginably bleak time.

Yes, I have been through a lot, but nowhere near as much as others. I feel so unbelievably grateful to have had these three heroes in my life.

I want to offer some contrast and to reiterate my struggle. My old perspective was one of reaction, overwhelm and often, borderline panic.

In the early days, I would feel dread and automatically fear the worst when I saw an email land in my inbox from someone I didn't really like, or someone I perceived was out to be a pain. In all manner of situations, I would automatically fear the worst. I was always looking for the bad and making up elaborate scenarios in my head.

I let the negative self-talk in. My perspective was all wrong. I focussed on what did not matter and allowed automatic thoughts to dominate.

With my new perspective, I now assess a situation and ask myself, *"Is it really that bad?"* and usually it isn't, so I can move on without the fear or drama.

In 2016 and 2017, when my Dad was in hospital, all wired up to machines and monitors. I remember having profound chats with him about life in general. My Dad and I could chit-chat and put the world to rights all day long! He had so much common sense and a brilliant perspective.

I remember him saying that the only regrets he had were about not doing more of the things that he wanted to, or going to places he wanted to go. Work always had to come first to fund us girls, so he didn't get to do all he wanted to do. Initially, this made me sad, but then it made me determined to do all the things I wanted to do and go to all those places, so that, if I died tomorrow, I could genuinely say I had lived a full, balanced and great life. They say 'collect moments, not things' and this is what I do now.

If it all went away tomorrow, can you, hand on heart, say that you are on the right path to being happy? If not, what can you change to get you there?

Never forget that what you have today isn't guaranteed for tomorrow; so, don't take situations, people or your health for granted. Keep in mind that it can all change in a positive way, too. When you live your life with this in mind, it is amazing how you flourish and how you see things in such a different and powerful way.

Action Step:

In your Mindset Workbook, turn to The Perspective section. The idea of this exercise is to establish what really matters to you. In the spider diagram entitled, 'What Really Matters to Me" let your thoughts flow and just write what feels right. Don't judge your thoughts, just let them come.

Then, when you've done that, turn to the 'What Really *Doesn't* Matter to Me' spider diagram and start writing anything that enters your head. You can keep coming back to this if you need to.

Chapter 10

Looking Downstream

So we know that focussing on what matters and looking the other way can change everything for us. I hope from Chapter 9 that you felt how profound perspective was, and still is, for me, and how it shaped my life. Perhaps it sparked a few thoughts in your mind about your own life and ways you can change your perspective.

Building on perspective, I want to talk to you about a metaphor I discovered whilst out walking the dog in May 2017; a metaphor which has now become an integral part of my daily life and has influenced many of my decisions.

I live in a beautiful village in a quiet corner of Shropshire. It's quintessentially English with a handful of independent shops and pubs. My village is surrounded by the most idyllic countryside – perfect for walking the dog and just clearing your mind.

Most days, I walk the dog down by the river which lies in the bottom of a tree-lined valley. There's a footbridge I quite often sit on. It's such a great place to go to gather my thoughts. You know those places that just feel right to you? This is mine. It is pure peace and quiet and there is no phone signal down there either, which makes it even more special.

In the summer, when my Dad was ill, I often went to the river for some 'me' time and to get my energy levels up. I would always sit down and face upstream. Even though it was tranquil and serene down in that spot, it always felt a little frantic when I looked upstream because the water was racing downstream and crashing against the rocks.

One day I went down there and I sat facing the other way. It was only a subtle change of direction, but in doing that I got an entirely different view of the water. As the water went under the bridge it flowed away calmly, there were no rocks or rapids like there were upstream. I thought of the river as my thoughts and when I looked downstream everything seemed to just flow easier within me. The resistance wasn't there; instead a sense of ease.

It occurred to me in that moment that I had been "facing" the wrong way. It was that simple, all I had to do was to look a different way to get a totally different experience. That was it, my metaphor was reframing, looking downstream for ease instead of upstream for stress or difficulty.

This metaphor about reframing was so simple, yet so profound to me. It was, once again, a lesson to never underestimate the power of a single moment which can change your life. Always be on the look-out for those moments.

In that moment, I realised that everything was all about mindset. I stayed down by the river for a while, looking downstream and I thought about how this related to my struggle. I thought about how hard I had made things for myself in the early years of the S&CBC; how I created the hardship. I created all the resistance around me, but now I saw a powerful way to change everything. I suddenly saw the power of reframing.

In its absolute simplest form, all I had to do was look the other way for a totally different experience. I was keen to test out my metaphor and to see if it was that simple. I also wanted to test my theory, to see if it was just all about changing your mind to change your life.

Looking downstream (reframing) applied to my grief too. During 2018, I can, hand on heart, say that reframing changed my life. As the sadness became more manageable, I chose to use my grief in a positive way. I could have let it define me and I could have plunged into despair but, instead, I used it for good. My Dad was so proud of me. I knew he was. I knew I had to take the lessons and look for the good.

I also know he would be even more proud of me now as an

author! As I went forward in my life without him, I had to look for the good. I reframed it all and, as a result, the entire trajectory of my life changed.

TRUTH BOMB: Even the simplest of actions have power. Never underestimate them!

As the months went on and things played out around me, I committed to reframing and changing my mindset. As with perspective, I chose to look at what was important and to let go of what was not. Things really started to open up for me. I felt better, stronger and just more settled in; fewer things bothered me too, which was so freeing.

Reframing really helped me go from seeing a loss to a gain. It helped me go from seeing lack, to abundance. It enabled me to see solutions instead of problems. It helped me see how strong I was after losing my Dad, instead of how helpless. Most importantly, it helped me see the impossible as possible. It helped me to see a way out of the stress filled cycle I was in. It helped me to see a setback as a step forward and it helped me see that I'm on the right path now. Aside from all that, it makes me feel really empowered and in control. Reframing stops me feeling stuck. It helps me rise and move forward.

Reframing allows me to change the meaning of something that makes me react. It gives me a choice, instead of just a reaction. I can choose between letting a situation make me feel reactive or, in the case of my new downstream way, I can reframe it to something positive.

It gave me my power back. As a result, I saved time by choosing not to be reactive. Time which I would previously have spent on self-pity or feeling resentful, was now available for me to be happy and grateful, and to just enjoy myself.

Like with all of my journey to balance, I made reframing a part of my life through small but consistent changes. My mindset journey is a continual process and I knew that reframing was only one part of the puzzle.

There was always a lot stress in the early years of my business, with a heightened focus on the problems and the negatives which, of course, was not conducive to balance. I think a little bit of pressure can make you productive, but I didn't have just a little bit of pressure; tons of it pushed down on me. I had come so far on my mindset journey, but I knew I still had some work to do. I had to switch my default mood. It required me to see a new way of doing things and focus on all the good, in whatever form that took.

I often keep going back to the phrase, *"where focus goes, energy flows"*. The more we look at something, the more of that we get. When we reframe and focus on a more positive perspective, our vibration rises.

A disclaimer: I am not saying always quash your feelings and never feel annoyed, fed up, or angry. I am saying look at things another way and you will benefit with good feeling. That good feeling will change your life, just like it has done for me.

One of the first things I needed to reframe were grudges. I have wasted a lot of time holding grudges. There were some people I used to feel so angry about, that just thinking about them would make my heart race.

I thought holding a grudge was fine, but it really is not. Holding onto toxic feelings and emotions is not balanced, as it is only really you who suffers in the end. The person you have the grudge against doesn't always know you have it, so it doesn't affect them, which makes your grudge pointless.

By holding onto bad feelings, you are blocking good feelings and holding on to what doesn't matter, instead of what does and that is a shame. You are wasting energy that you could be spending on something more meaningful to you. There is an old saying that holding a grudge is like drinking a vial of poison and expecting the other person to die.

You do not have to physically make peace with someone who has wronged you, but make peace with them in your mind and move on. I reframed some of my grudges, which really freed me up and I felt so much better by letting them go. If you are not ready to forgive, then block, delete and forget. Rise above, head held high, and let it go. Don't use your energy where it is not appreciated or deserved.

Here are a few examples of Upstream vs Downstream thoughts:

Situation: You want to do something bold that pushes your comfort zone. Something that is big, different or potentially uncomfortable. The gain is set to be big, should you do it?

Upstream thought: Your inner voice tells you all the reasons why you can't do it. Who are you to do that, anyway? Doing things like this isn't for people like you. It'll be too hard and too uncomfortable. Just don't bother, it's too hard.

Downstream thought: You know it's just your ego talking. How will you ever know what it's like if you don't try it? How amazing will you feel if you achieve what it is you want? Doing it may be the catalyst for pushing your comfort zone even further. Think of the confidence it'll bring you.

Situation: You have created some amazing work and put it online. The next day, you see that someone has pretty much impersonated you to the letter!

Upstream thought: You feel frustration, betrayal and it might cut you deep. You might want to seek revenge, tell the world, publicly confront and call the perpetrator out.

Downstream thought: It's actually a huge compliment that someone has imitated you. You feel validated that what you have put out is very good and you feel proud to be an inspiration. Only you have your unique slant and value proposition, so theirs won't be the same. You acknowledge that there are more than enough customers to go around, so it's no biggie. Plus, you got in there first!

*Situation***:** A friend has been intentionally unkind to you for no reason.

Upstream thought: Anger, revenge and retaliation. You might want to be unkind back and put them in their place.

Downstream thought: Compassion. They obviously have something going on that has made them react like this. It's not you; it's them. They are likely venting. What can you do to support them? Or, perhaps you can remove yourself from the situation.

If you have been looking upstream for too long, I want to reiterate the impact it can have on your day. When we allow ourselves to react and look upstream (be reactive / negative), we tend to hold onto those feelings and they often escalate. When we do this, there is a good chance we will allow the negativity to hijack our whole day. You might well carry those feelings of anger forward and it is such a waste. It might make you feel resentful and reclusive. My point is, we need to get over it. ASAP. There is a lot of good going on around us and the sooner we can let things go, the better. Like attracts like, so if you are harbouring toxic thoughts, you are going to get more of those.

I know when people wrong us, it can be all-consuming and hurtful. By looking upstream, we are only compounding the impact on ourselves though – not on them. If we choose the downstream way, we can let it go, move on, and keep moving forward without letting it impact on us. It is up to us. It is our choice.

For me, it is about good feelings every time. I have wasted a lot of time on things that did not matter.

Reframing the past

Some of us struggle with things we have done or that have happened to us in the past. Maybe there is something you did that still makes you feel regret or hold on to. Often things that have gone still hold power over us and we still feel uncomfortable about them. I had a few of these things which I really held onto over the years, which affected my self-worth. If there are small things you can release from your past with reframing, do it; let go of those uncomfortable feelings and set yourself free.

Say for instance, you did something when you were growing up and looking back, you still feel bad. Can you find some good to take away from it? For instance, has that guilt made you a better person?

Aside from the not-so-nice feelings, perhaps it has made you never want to do it again. Maybe you have inadvertently upped your game because of it. Good can come from every bad situation, depending on how we look at it. Look downstream, take from it what you can, and then move forward.

Reframing is such a useful tool that I have used for all manner of things; from instances where people have been unkind, to my own confidence, grief and much more. Once you start reframing, it becomes so much easier and quicker to deal with things emotionally. And once you start to see the subtle benefits as I did, you'll want to keep doing it.

TRUTH BOMB: Consistent small shifts add up to big changes.

Action Step: In your Workbook, turn to the Downstream section

Think of a situation that has been playing on your mind or that isn't sitting right with you. Write the situation at the top. Sometimes, even just writing something out and facing it can make it lose its power. Then, in the left-hand column, list all the negative, upstream things and feelings – anger, jealousy and any other emotions. Write them all down.

Then, in the right-hand column, write a counterpoint, an upstream and positive reaction for each negative. Write how you would deal with them if you were in a downstream frame of mind.

Then, take some time to think about the positives and how they benefit you. Reframe the situation, breathe it in, then let it go and move forward with your life. I used to do this exercise a lot. As time goes on, you won't need to write it down.

Action: Let us know in the Facebook Group what you are reframing, or if you need help in reframing.
Challenge: To take it one step further, make a commitment to look downstream every day for a week. See what happens, see how you feel and how your week changes. Keep at it!

When you are in alignment and things just feel 'right", you can live a life of freedom and happiness. Going from burnt out and frazzled and trying to be Wonder Woman just doesn't work. Incremental changes are where it's at. Small moves such as reframing add up and become habits. When you have strong, positive habits, the magic happens. Little by little, step by step, day by day.

Bonus Point: If you are holding onto a grudge that you need to let go of, write the person involved a letter. (Note: You don't have to give it them).

Open a Google Doc or your journal and write all the reasons why you have your grudge. Write how they made you feel, write how you have reframed it all, and how you have forgiven them. Get it all out, makes you cry. Have a good purge, then hit delete.

Now, breathe. You have such a great journey ahead of you and you do not need any unnecessary baggage. You must protect your precious energy and remember what is important.

Chapter 11

Gratitude

TRUTH BOMB: Everything is about how you feel, not what you have

So you know how bringing gratitude into my daily life changed everything and how it came right when I needed it. From that state of appreciation, my life began to open up in new ways. I looked for the positives in everything, I was nicer to be around and just in general. I also felt so much happier and stronger. It's as if I can handle most things, instead of dreading everything like I used to. For instance, when something happens now which isn't ideal, I default to gratitude as opposed to flying off the handle! Of course I do still get annoyed or angry, but I nearly always choose to see the good first. My happiness is more important to me than running someone down or holding a grudge. I have spent too much time doing that already. This was a massive shift for me, keeping perspective and putting my happiness first, it's amazing what falls away, or what you no longer care about when you do that.

Feeling kinder and happier definitely made me feel more enriched. My life had gone from slog, to enjoyment. New people started showing up in my world who were on the same path. I think when you are kinder and more appreciative, those around you can't help but reciprocate. Gratitude has had a massive impact on me and it has benefitted my loved ones too, as I am so much nicer to be around. We are all just a bit nicer, more forgiving and more loving when we are grateful – everyone steps up.

It is your right as a human being to be happy. You owe it to yourself, and to those who love you, to feel as good as you can every single day. When you feel good, you are great fun to be around (and who doesn't want to be like that?). You become more inspiring and people are drawn to you. You are enthusiastic, animated and people love being in your company. I know this first hand, as people often take the trouble to tell me.

We all know those people who are radiant and make us feel like a million dollars and we just want to be near them – I know I do! You are totally one of those people, we all are. Chances are life has just got on top of you, people got you down and you forgot how to sparkle. Gratitude, in my view, gives you that sparkle back – it definitely gave mine back to me.

Just like with perspective and reframing, it is about committing to gratitude and being consistent, as that is where the big change happens.

We all know that we can't get away from bad things happening to us. If I could have avoided three deaths of people I adored in nine months, trust me, I would. Things will always happen to derail us and push our boundaries – that's ok, as we don't have to be totally chipper all the time. Just 10 per cent more than usual, then maybe 20 per cent more than you were before. Little changes add up.

Also, many of us overcomplicate things and unintentionally cause drama around ourselves. I was the Queen of this in my struggle – seeing problems as an attack on me or my efforts. The key is how we deal with it all – how we control our reactions and make it work for us. I hope I am living proof that it is possible.

If you are not convinced of the power of gratitude, I want to share some scientific research with you. There are hundreds of studies out there about gratitude, but these are a few of my favourites:

The 2003 study of Counting Blessings Vs Burdens.
The study revealed that subjects who kept a gratitude journal reported a 25% improvement in sleep quality. The subjects did 19% more exercise than usual and reported 10% less

physical pain.
Isn't that incredible? Just from feeling grateful.

The Department of Psychology at Southern Methodist University in Dallas did a study.
The study showed that gratitude gives us a positive memory bias. This means when we experience gratitude and practice it daily, we are more likely to recall the most positive memories from our past. It makes negative memories appear less intense.

If you are feeling anxious or depressed, then this one is for you:

A 2014 study published in Aging and Mental Health showed that participants who practiced gratitude showed a significant decrease in anxiety and depression. This was as well as an increase in specific memories, life satisfaction and subjective happiness, compared with the placebo group.

If you are not convinced, or if gratitude seems a bit out there for you, here are some more life-changing, proven benefits:

- Gratitude boosts productivity.
- Gratitude gives you more energy and helps you sleep better.
- Gratitude makes you a better leader and inspires others.
- Gratitude gives you more meaning to life and makes you kinder.
- Gratitude reduces stress.
- Gratitude boosts your willpower and optimism.
- Gratitude makes you happier about your life and increases satisfaction.
- Gratitude boosts your mental health, while decreasing anxiety and depression.

- Gratitude makes your immune system and heart stronger.

When we are stressed, our bodies release a fight or flight hormone called cortisol. Hands up, I am sure in the early years of my business that my body must have always been awash with cortisol. When we feel stressed, we keep getting hits of cortisol, which depletes energy from our bodies. This in turn causes our immune system to weaken and, as a result, we get ill. So, by keeping positive and grateful, we keep our cortisol levels in check and our bodies healthier, and instead we release hits of feel-good hormones serotonin and dopamine. How good is that? We physically get ill less.

A 2012 study published in 'Personality and Individual Differences' found that gratitude improved health. *It said people who are grateful tend to have fewer aches and pains, and generally felt healthier than other people. Grateful people are more likely to look after their health too. They exercise more often and are more likely to attend regular medical check-ups.* All good stuff. I know I have really started to look after my health more since being more grateful.

The University of Southern California said in a study that: *"Gratitude is likely a side effect of reduced stress. Those who practice gratitude have a 16 per cent lower diastolic blood pressure and a 10 per cent lower systolic blood pressure than those who don't."*

So we know the proven benefits of gratitude – what else? Gratitude has enabled me to feel as though I can get through anything. It allows us to hold moments in the present and appreciate where we are and what we have. It's about being present, not being on your phone and not worrying or thinking ahead about things you can't control. It's about enjoying what you are doing and who you are with in that moment.

Have you lived in the present lately? When was the last time you put your phone away and looked around to see all of the good in your world?

There is no right or wrong way to be grateful. I am going to share with you how I can be in this state for so much of my life.

You might follow my path, or you might find your own. The goal – no matter how you get to it – is to find that feeling of gratitude. The feeling of love, appreciation, possibility and joy.

If this sounds weird or unfamiliar, I want to share a little exercise with you to help bring out that feeling. This is something you can do anywhere or anytime. This is one of my quick wins. I love a quick win!

Put your hand on your heart, close your eyes and think about something you are grateful for. It could be your family, a pet, or something that you can't live without. Can you really feel how much you love them? Really feel it in your heart and then radiate it into your chest.

That is the feeling you want. You can apply this feeling to all sorts of things. You might feel grateful just for the quiet time you are having reading this book. Perhaps you are grateful for what a beautiful day it is.

Once you have the grateful feeling, take a few deep breaths and let that feeling grow. Breathe it in and feel it in your heart. You can hold that feeling for ten seconds or a few minutes – do what feels good for you. Let that feeling grow in you. Once you have felt it, do it again and again. It is addictive. I bring this feeling on so many times throughout the day and just let it wash over me. I do have so much to be grateful for and it's lovely to remind myself of it.

A biological change happens when we put our hands on our hearts. It releases oxytocin, which is known as the love drug! New Mums who breastfeed their babies experience surges of oxytocin. It makes us bond, gives us pleasure and just makes us feel good. The super simple practice of putting your hand on your heart and feeling love gives us a hit of the love drug.

Try it as soon as you wake up, while you are still in bed – put your hand on heart and activate that grateful feeling. Have a hand on your heart when you brush your teeth, when you are on the phone, or doing anything at all! It is subtle, but the more you do it, the more powerful it becomes.

If you are thinking this all sounds a bit unattainable, I want to reassure you that it's ok. We all have off days. There are days when

I want to stay in bed, watch Netflix, and eat ice-cream – and that is fine. Being balanced affords us that from time to time. Even if you are feeling a bit out of sorts or just frustrated, you can still be grateful. I really encourage you to put pen to paper and journal, and put your hand on your heart. If nothing else, you will feel like you have achieved something.

Remember the pre-grateful me? The ratty, worn out and not-fun-to-be-around version of me? My focus was on stress and that is where all my energy was going. The more I focussed on stress, the more of it I experienced.

When I flipped to gratitude, I had more reasons to be grateful. Hopefully now can you see that, by investing this time in myself and my mood every day, my focus has shifted and my life has changed.

Start small with gratitude and see where it takes you.

Affirmations

You may do them already, or you may have seen people who stand in front of a mirror repeating a positive statement while they are brushing their teeth – *"I am strong and capable,"* or *"I am worthy and enough"*. These are positive affirmations. It is a statement you say, write, or think repeatedly, which helps your brain bring it to reality.

Affirmations are a little hack with powerful results on a neural level in our brains. They are positive statements that, when we repeat them daily, have huge effects. An affirmation effectively tricks our brains to believe that it is true, or that it has already happened, even if it hasn't. On a basic level, affirmations help us reprogramme our thought patterns by creating new neural pathways in our brains. By affirming what we want several times, we will start to feel like we can achieve it. Plus, our Reticular Activation Syetem will come into play and we will start noticing events or signs that support what it is we want and need.

You can use affirmations for any area of your life where you want to make change. You can use them for losing weight, self-confidence, to stop smoking, achieve goals – anything. I have used affirmations a lot over the past few years. I have used them for getting through my grief, for changing the structure of the S&CBC, for launching the LSC and even writing this book.

According to the Chopra Centre, this is what happens when you use positive affirmations:

- You become aware of your daily thoughts and words, reducing the risk of letting negativity seep in.
- You notice more synchronicities in your life, which serves to encourage and motivate you to keep up the practice.
- Daily affirmations not only help keep you surrounded by the things you want in your life, but they help bring about more blessings and gifts.
- A daily practice helps to keep the small things in perspective. In this high-speed world, you can easily lose sight of how large the small things really are. When you are healthy, you may forget to think of how much you appreciate it. A simple morning affirmation sentence of *"I am healthy"* can go a long way.
- A recent study shows that optimistic people have healthier hearts and affirmations help you to stay positive.
- As you continue this practice, others take notice and you begin to help those around you without even trying. This, in turn, helps keep you focussed.
- Daily affirmations keep you in a constant state of gratitude.

When it comes to choosing your positive affirmations, create them to suit you. You can of course use ready-made ones, or something that resonates with you. I tend to create my affirmations around my goals or how I want to feel.

Really important: Your affirmations must be in the present tense. They must contain statements of truth or fact. This means you should not use the words 'could, should or might etc'. Uber decisive and sure is the way to go. The main thing here is that they must resonate with you and be believable.

Action step:

In your workbook or your notebook, write down five things that you are grateful for right now. If you want to write more than five then great, keep writing all of the things you are grateful for. Read them back and cultivate that feeling with your hand on your heart. How incredible is your life right now?

Next, create three affirmations that feel good and are written in the present. Write them in your journal, say them in the shower every morning and really start believing them.

Bonus: Create a recurring reminder on your phone to prompt you to feel grateful, even if it's just for thirty seconds. Stick some post-it notes around your house saying *"What am I grateful for?"* or one of your affirmations. We know we can create a new habit in a short time. If you start now, imagine how great you are going to be feeling a month from now!

Chapter 12

Quieting Your Mind And

Imagining It Done

When was the last time you sat down for five minutes, on your own, phone on silent, with no distractions? I am talking pure "me time" – can you even remember? I know I never used to and it really showed with my struggle. Because my mind was always racing, I could never really settle into what I was doing or get into a flow state. Taking time for yourself, even if it's just five minutes here and there, is a necessity. During these sacred moments you decompress, recharge and receive your best thoughts. For me having quiet time became a habit which lead to a much more content and balanced way of life.

Why don't you just stop right now only for a minute? Close your eyes and take some deep breaths and just totally stop everything. In through your nose and out through your mouth. Just offload whatever it is you have going on. Breathe it in and then let it go.

Being connected to people we love, admire, and are inspired by is amazing, but now so much of our life is lived online and there is so much digital noise and notifications. It's exhausting if we don't manage it and are constantly trying to keep up with all of the updates. There is no getting away from how accessible we are in this digital age and that is great most of the time, but we all feel the downsides of always being available.

Let's start with the barrage of notifications to stay on top of:

what people's dogs have done, or then there are the dinner posts, the people ranting at strangers posts, there's the rabbit hole we get embroiled in arguments about comments on things on Facebook – it is tiring and so much of it is unnecessary. This is before I have even mentioned our obligations on and offline. On top of that, there is the seemingly never-ending dialogue and doubt we have going on in our heads, which I call negative chatter. Whilst it is great to be connected, and the self-talk is sometimes useful in terms of reminding us about things, most of the time, it is simply exhausting.

TRUTH BOMB: Overthinking and being overburdened causes us to be overwhelmed

I have had to adjust my life and quiet my mind an awful lot to get me to this place where I am now. There are a few things I have had to do to quieten my mind:

- Quieten down the habit of endlessly going over my to-do list in my head. I now do this by just writing it all down.
- Quieten the doubt and physical distractions, by managing my phone time, and applying structure and boundaries.

I'm sure you have whole lists of things that you need to calm down in your mind, but my point is that it all needs quietening down. When we identify what needs to happen, we can achieve it with ease.

For me, I gave myself peace and quiet, which then became life-changing in terms of how I felt. I felt calmer, more patient, more in control and just more capable.

It makes me a little bit sad that it's the norm that so many of us are constantly glued to our phones or screens. It also makes me sad that so many of us spend so much time comparing ourselves to strangers on the internet. By doing this, we are missing out on real life moments with the ones we love. What if you could just stop the mental chatter, the fear of missing out and the comparisons for a day, then another day, then another day? What small changes would you have to make to do that?

TRUTH BOMB: You cannot get precious moments back, so make memories like your life depends on it!

Because I have put the work in and made the micro changes to my life, I now know that I can step away from the 'noise' in my life whenever I want to. It's like a mini reset. I take myself off somewhere quiet, close my eyes and focus on my breathing for a few minutes and it really hits my reset button – it reinvigorates me. I know that my own peace of mind and sanity is paramount and I can't do my best work if I am mentally all over the place. I make time to be quiet every day.

On average, we have somewhere between fifty thousand to eighty thousand thoughts every day. It's no wonder we can feel pushed and pulled in so many directions. The good news is that many of those thoughts are repeated from the day before, and the day before that. We call these automatic thoughts. Every day actions become automatic. A big chunk of these thoughts are the routine things we have conditioned ourselves to do, such as getting up, taking a shower, putting the coffee on and driving to work. We don't really think about doing these things consciously; we just do them.

Then there are automatic thoughts we have created that talk us into or out of things. I like to file these under the title of 'negative chatter'. Negative chatter to me is the untruths we tell ourselves that keep us stuck, keep us playing small and hold us back. Automatic and negative thoughts tell us we are not confident or are unworthy or incapable. You know the ones! We need to be aware of these automatic thoughts because then we can identify them and change them. It's about learning to change the dialogue with yourself. When we have negative automatic thoughts, reframing is effective. I often go a little deeper and use my 'What's the evidence?' exercise described below to rationalise the attempted negative self talk.

TRUTH BOMB: You are so incredibly precious to so many people. If only you could begin to see and believe it

When the negative chatter kicks in, we can shut it down in a few ways. By asking myself, 'What is the evidence?' I have learnt to quieten my mind.

Here is an example of a negative dialogue:

Negative you: *"No one really cares about what your business does. You might as well just give up. You'll never do any good."*

Impartial you: *"Where's the evidence?"*

Positive you: *"There isn't any evidence. I have really engaged followers who love my work. My sales stats are solid and I have many kind emails from happy customers. There is no solid fact that says no one cares."*

When you get down to the core of negative chatter, there is usually nothing to it. Once we know we can quieten it down and let it go, those thoughts should quieten.

Negative chat to me also ties back to perspective and reframing. What is more important to you: achieving your goals, or listening to what you know not to be true? You are the boss and, ultimately, you are in control. You only get one shot at life, so you might as well make it the best you can!

I think it is really important to swap disempowering thoughts for empowering statements. Swapping statements such as, *"I'm so busy. I feel like my head is going to explode,"* to something more positive like, *"I've made so much progress today. I'm so productive, capable and I feel so calm and accomplished."* By doing this, you are moving the thought to empowerment. Remember like attracts like. Stress attracts stress. Being empowered attracts more empowered thoughts.

TRUTH BOMB: You are far too special to be the only thing standing in your way

Meditation

Meditation, I am sure is one of the most powerful things you can do for your mental health. I wish I had taken this more seriously years ago. Taking time to just quieten your mind keeps you focussed and balanced. Meditation was helpful to me when I was coming out of my struggle, and it really helped me cope with my Dad's illness. It has now become a part of my daily life and I really notice when I don't do it. All my best thoughts and ideas come from being in a calm and focussed state.

If the thought of meditation freaks you out a little bit, then that's cool. It is one of those things you need to try for yourself. Meditation, like gratitude, has a phenomenal impact on our minds. If you need a little persuasion and are new to meditation, I want to share a list compiled by Emma M. Seppälä Ph.D. Emma is an associate director at Stanford University and author of *"The Happy Track"*. Dr Emma shared 20 scientifically validated reasons why we should all get into meditation. Meditation, like gratitude, can be life-changing as it comes with all these benefits:

- Increases immune function
- Decreases pain
- Decreases inflammation at a cellular level
- Increases positive emotion
- Decreases depression
- Decreases anxiety
- Decreases stress
- Increases social connection and emotional intelligence
- Makes you more compassionate
- Makes you feel less lonely
- Improves your ability to regulate your emotions
- Improves your ability to introspect

- Increases grey matter in your brain
- Increases volume in areas related to emotion regulation, positive emotions and self-control
- Increases cortical thickness in areas related to paying attention
- Increases your focus and attention
- Improves your ability to multitask
- Improves your memory
- Improves your ability to be creative and think outside the box
- Makes you wiser

There are so many scientific studies out there which highlight many, many more positive benefits of meditation. If you have never meditated before, then hopefully this list will encourage you to give it a go.

Just for the record, meditation is no longer a woo-woo or "*hippy*" activity. People like you and I are realising the benefits and getting on board with it. All the top entrepreneurs and elite athletes are making it part of their daily practice and they too are seeing the results. It is a powerful tool and it has personally helped me overcome such a lot. Meditation has become a non-negotiable part of my day. I started with two minutes a day – literally, that was it. I now do fifteen minutes a day. Once a week, I will do a half an hour guided meditation to really get me in the zone, but that is just my preference. Sometimes it will be first thing, or maybe just before lunch, or when I feel a bit frazzled, or simply just when I need it.

You don't have to do the full-on Buddhist route – unless of course you want to. A few minutes to yourself, here and there, when you can. It is the easiest thing to do and here is how you do it:

- Set a timer on your phone if you want to. You can start with just a few minutes.
- Make sure you are sitting comfortably where you won't be disturbed.
- Close your eyes and take a few deep breaths, in

through your nose, out through your mouth. Then, let your breathing find its natural pattern.

- Focus on your breath. Focus your attention on the air going in through your nose and out through your mouth.
- If thoughts keep coming into your mind, that's fine. Acknowledge each thought, let each thought go and bring your attention back to your breath.
- When your mind wanders, bring your attention back to your breathing.

The goal isn't a completely blank mind as that is totally off putting, but rather focussing on your breath and allowing thoughts to come and go. It's about quieting the noise and focussing on your breathing. If you are new and need some help, have a look for a short guided meditation on YouTube. Or you could start with an app like Calm or Headspace.

When you first start meditating – or quieting your mind, whichever you prefer to call it – chances are your conscious mind will try to tell you all sorts of things. Thoughts will pop into your head, like things you need to do, conversations you have had, or that you have an itch! All these thoughts are fine. Just let them drift in and out of your consciousness. Then, bring your attention back to your breathing. It really is that simple. There's no trick to it and we don't need to overcomplicate it.

As you practice more often and it becomes more natural, look at increasing the amount of time you devote to it. Ten minutes at either end of your day can change your life. If you take just two things from this book, make it meditation and gratitude. If you do try it – and I highly recommend that you do – please let me know how you get via our Facebook Group or my Instagram.

Visualisation

On a really simplistic level (without all of the limits life puts on us) we literally have the power to decide who or what we want to become. Our minds are the most phenomenal tools; we can make what we want a reality. Visualisation allows us to imagine things we want to achieve and connect to the feeling of what it feels like, then bring it into reality. As with affirmations, your brain cannot tell the difference between what is real or what is imagined. Therefore, we can make what we want real. I think we should all be visualising what we want every day. Visualisation puts our desires into our experience.

Visualisation is a performance enhancer. Our brains interpret the imagery we are creating in our mind's eye as fact. The brain creates messages to instruct us to carry out the actions that we want that we are visualising. So, as far our brains are concerned, our goals are a done deal. Oprah Winfrey uses it, Mohammed Ali did, high performers in business use it, as do elite athletes and even people with life-changing injuries.

Like with affirmations, research has shown that visualisation creates new neural pathways in our brains. When we focus on what we want, the chemistry in our brain changes. Our minds start to create a new neural pathway to help us achieve our desires. In short, we are creating a blueprint for our goals. This improves the likelihood of achieving what we want. Isn't that phenomenal!

I want to quickly touch on neuroplasticity, as this is a subject which fascinates me. Neuroplasticity means your brain can change its actual structure based on thought. Plasticity in this context means to change shape or rewire. An example of neuroplasticity is how the brain grows in certain areas when we master something. It also involves repairing old or damaged brain cells, reorganising the networks and pathways of feeling, imagining and dreaming etc.

It blows me away when I think that our brains can change physiologically when we believe something or master a new skill. Also that we can change our lives through changing our thoughts.

I want to share with you a study around visualisation. A psychologist from the Cleveland Clinic in Ohio called Dr Guang Yue did a study on gym goers. Half of the group of subjects went to the gym, while the other half of the group did virtual workouts in their minds. The results showed that the group who went to the gym had a 30% increase in muscle gain. This was as to be expected.

However, the visualisation control group, who didn't go near a gym, had a 13.5% increase in muscle gain, all from visualisation! Incredible isn't it? They didn't go near a gym, but their minds couldn't tell the difference between what was imagined and what was fact. New neural pathways were created which sent signals to the muscles, as if the subjects had been to the gym.

The key to effective visualisation is repetition and consistency. Rinse and repeat. The more you do it, the better you become at it, the more neural pathways are created, the more results you get. Your brain begins to reorganise itself to give you what you want. Like with any mindset practice, we are looking to create a strong positive emotion when we do it. Creating a strong positive emotion forces our brain to etch what we're visualising down as a memory.

I used visualisation when I was writing this book. I visualised how it felt to hold the finished book in my hands. I visualised what I would be doing, how I was feeling, where I was. I visualised it all in minute detail, including what I was seeing, feeling, hearing and smelling. I visualised people tagging me with a picture of them and my book on Instagram, saying how much they loved it! I created a strong positive emotion around that, which really spurred me on. I have also used it to visualise confidence, courage, calmness and other positive personality traits.

I have found that visualisation works best when my mind is quiet. So I always visualise immediately after my morning meditation.

Meditation and visualisation are the tools of Titans – just Google them if you want to find out more.

Action Step:

Quieten your mind and imagine it done.

1   Set a timer on your phone right now for three minutes and sit in absolute quiet, focussing on your breathing and close your eyes.

2   Set your timer for another three minutes and spend the time imagining it done. Use massive detail to see yourself achieving what it is that you want. Bring in all your senses.

3   If you have a lot on your mind that feels too much, write it all down.

Visualisation Inspiration:

- Big goals.
- Reinventing yourself.
- Having something you want.
- Being a different way (calm, more outgoing, confident)

Give your mind the instructions it needs to create what you want, then it will start to show you what you need to do to bring it into reality. Take note of any impulses, thoughts or great ideas you have when you are meditating too.

Challenge: Thirty days of meditation challenge!

Use the meditation sheet in your workbook and take five minutes wherever you can to quieten your mind.

Tick off every day you meditate and share a photo in our Facebook Group or on Instagram using the hashtag #MakeItHappenBook when you have ticked off all 30 days.

Chapter 13

Journaling And Clearing The Decks

Like meditation, journaling is one of those massively transformational tools that took me a while to cotton on to, but that I now get
massive benefits from.

Journaling has helped me to make sense of many things over the
past few years. I have solved some of my biggest challenges and
faced some of my biggest fears in my journal. I have talked myself
into things I had previously talked myself out of. In it, I have realised my worth, I have gained clarity and I have counselled myself
through loss. Everything is in my journal.

To me, our journals are a place where we can go deep on our
feelings and inner-most thoughts without the fear of being judged
by anyone. It is a safe space where we can make sense of things and
work things out.

Journaling is my final mindset strategy. Combine it with gratitude, reframing, meditation and visualisation and we can get
through most things. Trust me! Journaling to me is different to
gratitude journaling. I do gratitude journaling in single points,
whereas journaling is about letting your thoughts flow and writing
as much as you like. It can be whatever you want it to be. Journaling is especially powerful for those who aren't as vocal as me with
their emotions and thoughts.

In this chapter, we are going to look at journaling first. Then we
are going to get into clearing the decks and making more emotional
space for yourself. To me it has been so important to allow myself
more mental bandwidth by letting go of emotional clutter. Once you

have more space mentally, you have more space for better feelings and thoughts.

TRUTH BOMB: When you let go of the old, you make space for the new

There are so many reasons why journaling is such a powerful tool. I want to share these studies with you which illustrate that.

A 2005 study by Karen A. Baikie and Kay Wilhelm at Cambridge found that expressive writing connected with journaling is therapeutic. The study found that participants who wrote about traumatic, stressful, or emotional events, were significantly less likely to become sick. They were also less seriously affected by trauma, than their non-journaling counterparts.

Lead researcher at The University of Texas and author of *Writing to Heal*, James W. Pennebaker, has found that by translating our experiences into our own language, by writing it out, we are able to make the experience more comprehendible.

Kathleen Adams, a psychotherapist and author of *Journal to the Self*, said, "Journal therapy is all about using personal material as a way of documenting an experience and learning more about yourself in the process. It lets us say what's on our minds and helps us get – and stay – healthy through listening to our inner desires and needs."

Isn't all that really powerful? I have four big reasons to share with you below on why journaling is one of my tried and tested mindset strategies. These of course will be the same for you, plus you might find your own benefits as you go along.

- Journaling lowers stress and overwhelm. When I write about what I have going on emotionally, it can lessen the intensity of whatever it is and I'm effectively committing any uncomfortable feelings to paper. This process reduces the power of any negative feelings. Instead of holding on to stress or uncomfortable feelings all day, I'm offloading it.

- Journaling helps me gain clarity. When I have a lot going on, I can work out a way forward in my journal. I've actually come up with some pretty amazing solutions and ways forward in my journal. It also helps me to rationalise and takes some of the pressure off my mind.
- Resolves issues or problems. Writing out problems enables me to use both my left and right brain. This helps me to come up with creative and intuitive solutions.
- Be more understanding: This is great for those times when you find yourself wound up or if you've had an argument with someone. Let your thoughts and feelings flow. Start to journal away any grudges you may have too.

I use journaling for two mains purposes. Firstly, I write how I'm feeling every day. This is fascinating to look back on and to see how my story has unfolded, plus what mattered to me in a certain moment. It's great to help me stay on track with my feelings, to stay aligned with my goals and where I'm headed. Also, when I feel I'm blocked by something, I'll journal my way out of a specific problem.

If you don't feel comfortable writing your deepest and darkest thoughts in a journal, that's ok. You can write them in a Google doc and then delete it once you have offloaded it all. Include what the problem is, how it's making you feel and let your thoughts flow to how you can overcome the problem. What is the best possible outcome and how do you create it?

Clearing the decks

In order to lead a balanced life, we have to get rid of the old to allow in the new – the new being what we want now. To me, clearing the decks means making emotional space and getting rid of what no longer serves you. This includes old beliefs, old ways, unhelpful thoughts and anything that just weighs you down and holds you back. Just like keeping your house tidy, I genuinely believe you have to keep your mind tidy too.

In this section I'm going to talk to you about the following:

- Identifying negative/limiting beliefs.
- Emotional Freedom Technique (EFT).
- Clearing space around you.

We all have limiting beliefs and blocks about ourselves and the world around us. Limiting beliefs can come from anywhere.

When you were growing up, you may have been told to keep your head down and to find a proper job. Perhaps someone said you were weird or not good enough. You might have done some regrettable things in the past (we're all guilty of this). Maybe someone did something to you and now you find it hard to trust. Chances are you have had experiences which have held you back until this point and blocked you from achieving the greatness which you were born for, and which you owe to yourself.

The good news is, just like automatic thoughts, once we realise what a false belief or block is, we can manage it. I want to tell you more about my limiting beliefs.

When I launched the S&CBC, I had a major and unjust lack of self-confidence in what I was offering. I would lie awake at night and wonder what I was doing and go through tons of negative self-talk. It's such a good thing I am stubborn by nature, or I probably would have given up ten times over. The dialogue I would have with myself sounded something like this:

"Do women even want to go clay shooting?! If they did, why do you think they would want to go with you?"

"Everything in shooting is green, brown, and grey. What the hell are you trying to do with pink! You look ridiculous..."

"People are laughing at you. If there was a demand for women's only shooting clubs, surely there would have been one by now."

"You have no experience in business, you'll never last..."

"You are joking! Who the hell is going to spend money with you? You'll have to pay them to come to your events!"

Brutal isn't it? I am sure you have similar beliefs to this about yourself too. If you haven't, you should write a book and tell me your secret!

I had limiting belief stacked on top of limiting belief. It was ridiculous. You pull off one layer of limiting beliefs and there are another ten underneath. But once I addressed my blocks, the layers did come off and quite easily, too. Even though there was all this negative chatter in my head and all the reasons why I should just get a job, I always had faith. I had faith that, no matter what, I was always going to make this work and that what I was offering was valuable to people. I was just making it difficult and creating roadblocks for myself.

As the months went on, I had a ton of milestones and, with each one, I built on it and it gave me confidence.

Throughout my journey I held my nerve. I became courageous and I had more success than I thought possible. It is so important that we push through the lies we are telling ourselves – they don't serve us at all. Nowadays I can sense limiting beliefs and untruths a mile off, and I have faith in myself that I will get through them.

With a block, I start with reframing and look at the block from another way. I will visualise myself overcoming it. I will journal on what truth there is in it or what I'm afraid of, then I will just get on with it. If I can't get on with it, I will get some help in, whether that's by talking to someone or by other means.

I want to share four of the most common blocks as I see them:

- **Self-doubt:** You know my journey with doubt. Doubt robs so many talented people of creating the future they want. You can't lead a balanced life if you are always on the back foot and wrangling with your inner voice. You didn't come this far, to only come this far. Only you have your unique gifts and approach. Someone, somewhere needs to hear what you have to say or do.

TRUTH BOMB: Doubt is the thief of potential

- **Imposter syndrome:** This is a huge one for so many of us. I had this in a BIG way when I started the S&CBC. Imposter syndrome makes you feel like a fraud or incapable, even though there is evidence to show you are not. I pushed through it in the early days. When it creeps up on me now, I take some time to list out my achievements and gather evidence to show I am having success.
- **You have been burnt in the past:** This is a difficult one, as we've all been through different things and have been burnt in different ways. I can only speak about what I have been through. I know this stuff stays with us. Remember this: from adversity comes resilience and creativity. Eyes on the prize. Use the mindset tools to get through. Look for inspiration and role models who have been through something similar.
- **Money blocks:** When we don't have money, we experience all sorts of emotions. I know this first hand because, when I started out, I had nothing for the first few years. Not having the money to do what we want to do can stall us, but we can be creative and get by. It's amazing how resourceful we can be when it

comes down to it. Having tight cash flow might bring on feelings of being unworthy or second rate – not to mention anxiety. It all really changed for me when I let go of the feeling of lack. Feeling more abundant helped me become more abundant. When money stress strikes, focus on what you do have in other areas and create a plan to move towards money.

I am sure a few – if not all of these – relate to you and your life too, plus you are bound to have more of your own.

All our blocks come with a feeling. We need to feel another way and replace the strong negative associations with strong positive feelings. Put your hand on your heart and give yourself a rush of love and gratitude. Think of something that makes you feel good and let that feeling flow and expand. I have an action step to help you get through blocks at the end of this chapter.

I want to share 'Emotional Freedom Technique' or EFT with you. EFT, known as 'tapping' is a form of acupressure. Negative emotions are caused by a disruption in the body's energy system and EFT works to clear these. It is so easy and involves tapping with two fingers on your energy meridians (acupressure points). There are set points on the hands, head, face, collarbone and just down from your armpit (Google the EFT points!).

The long and short of EFT is you say what your problem is aloud, whilst tapping on the energy meridians. You follow your problem with saying, "*I deeply and completely love and accept myself*". The science behind EFT is trying to get over the root cause by sending kinetic energy to our system. It's a bit like overwriting the belief.

Here's an example of an EFT statement.

"Even though I have never written a book before and I have no idea if people will like it, it's fine, as I will gain so much from it myself. I deeply and completely love and accept myself."

EFT has been a game changer for me and it used to be a big part of my daily routine, now I just use it when I need it. You can literally do it for a minute, or you can do it more in depth and go for longer and really expand on a bigger limiting belief. You can even write yourself an EFT list if you want to go deep and clear all your blocks away. As with the other strategies, it's about consistency. Not sure how it looks? Have a look on YouTube for 'Tapping with Brad'.

Emotions and blocks aside, we need to be clearing the decks physically too. Tidy up! You can't do your best work in a mess or whilst distracted. If your workplace looks like a recycling centre, you need to clear it up and make it a beautiful space. Balanced women don't have a stash of dirty coffee cups, baskets of laundry, or half-eaten sandwiches on their desk.

Having a tidy space to work from is proven to boost productivity and to keep you feeling balanced. On my desk I have my laptop, some photos, my vision board hung up next to it, an A4 notebook to capture any great ideas and my planner. There is also a giant silver pineapple! Keeping your workspace clutter-free cuts down on distractions and gives you space to think and to create.

Clearing the decks is also self-care, and I cannot stress enough the importance of clearing space for ourselves.

To me it also means clearing the decks of people who sap your energy – in life or in business. This involves boundaries, but you must be careful with your time and energy. Both are so precious.

A final note on clearing the decks. Here's what I did:

- I did the internal work on losing as many blocks as I could. I did EFT on the big ones around doubt.
- I made journaling non-negotiable and wrote through my blocks. I explored my blocks and insecurities and wrote ways out of them, or why I was going to surrender them, and the steps I needed to take.
- I drastically cut down my social media time and stopped comparing myself to others.
- I let go of people in my business who I felt weren't in alignment and made space for the ones who were.
- I said goodbye to the big egos in my life, the energy

vampires and the time suckers. I said goodbye to situations and scenarios which didn't feel 'right' too.
- I gave myself time to get away and left guilt behind.
- I went outside more, which never fails to make me feel good.
- I allowed myself extra room for happiness.

We have new beliefs and blocks that come up all the time. As we move through the seasons in our lives, or reach the next level in what we want, there will be new challenges. This is a sure-fire sign of growth. As we reach new levels, we are equipped with tools to lessen the power of these new challenges.

Journal out what you can, clear some space for yourself and just know you've got this and you will get through it. If I can, you can!

Action Steps:

Blocks

Turn to the 'Blocks' page in your workbook and identify five big blocks that are keeping you stuck right now. Write out why you believe them so that you can get to the root of why they have power over you. Then, underneath each one, write down how and why you are going to overcome it. This is so simple, but sometimes it is the simplest solutions which are best. Just seeing the reality on paper is powerful.

Journaling Action

Open your journal and just write. It's up to you what you write and what comes to mind. Don't judge yourself or what you write; just let it flow.

Here are a few optional journal prompts for you:

- Write through your blocks and how you are relieving them of their power.
- Write about where you are right now and rationalise or reframe anything that feels uncomfortable to you.
- Write about where you are going or what your big goal is and how it's a done deal.
- Write about how excited you are that you are on this new path and affirm it.
- Write down all the reasons why you should quit your job or ditch the relationship that no longer serves you.
- Write why you are not waiting until you have lost the weight, saved the money, or had your hair done. Write about how ready you are now to make it happen!

Challenge: Join our seven-day journaling challenge and see how much better you feel. Head over to our Facebook Group and search for the #JournalChallenge post and comment to let us know you are in!

Include in your post where you are from, where you are in your business and what you are hoping to get out of it. It's amazing when we all support each other. If you are looking for an accountability partner, add that too.

- Tidy up your work area!
- Set a reminder in your phone or write a note to repeat this every day!

Chapter 14

A Balanced Mindset

By now I hope you are feeling a little more inspired and equipped to tackle life and all it serves up for you. Maybe you've already tried out some of the mindset tools. Maybe even you have had a go and it has prompted you to discover some of your own. Whatever you take from this part, I hope it helps you realise that we all have the power to change our own lives.

For me, even just knowing I have all of these mindset tools to come back to at any time helps me feel more in control and supported when I go off balance.

I've found that sometimes things are just so obvious, or so small or subtle, that we just discount them and we shouldn't! It's often the most simple things which are the most effective. Who knew you could get all this good by just making small but mighty, free shifts, every day? Plus it's all free and you can do it sat on your sofa.

Once you start to balance your outlook and commit to a new way, everything really does start to change. As I implemented the tools and strategies, slowly but surely, things felt calmer for me and opportunities started to open up for me. The more I felt tiny shifts within me and around me, the better I felt and the more I was ready to commit to this new way.

I think it's important to remind you that changing your mindset and your life is all about little steps and doing what's right for you. I think it's also important to realise that you'll never have it all done, whether that's your mindset or your day-to-day life. Always re-member life is continual and we're always growing, there's no final stop where we can say we've made it. We are constantly evolving, growing, learning and levelling up. The smoother we can make that journey through keeping our approach focussed, the better our lives become. Why wouldn't we want to make it as easy as we can for ourselves?

The importance of having a balanced mindset

A balanced mindset is about choosing to look for hope and the positive aspects first. It is creating space around you for 'me time'. It is about quieting the negative self-talk and amplifying the good. It is about being grateful and ambitious. It is knowing you can overcome anything and that you are stronger than you think.

TRUTH BOMB: When you start to believe you can overcome anything, that's when you become powerful enough to do it

This journey I have been on – striving for balance – has given me the confidence to back myself. I now have faith in myself and my abilities like never before and that is an amazing feeling to have.

I have faith that what will be, will be. I know whatever happens to me – no matter what is it – I can and will overcome it. The reality is that I might not achieve the desired outcome, as so much happens outside of our control, but I know I will deal with it. It may be tough or life-changing, but I know I can handle whatever arises. It is a bold statement to make, I know, but this is where I am at. Of course, there will be things that slap me down and test my resolve, but I will take the lessons and keep moving forward.

So, how did I get to this point? Honestly, it's just all down to repetition and creating new and positive habits, being consistent and remembering to actually do it too! In Part Three, we're going to start with creating your own Daily Success Routine so you can find ways to build a new, positive mindset and habits around your daily life. My hope for you is that, if you really want to change your life, you can, with belief and a framework or structure. I have the structure; you just need to bring the commitment and belief.

When it comes to self-belief, I think we should all stop apologising so much too. So many of us apologise for things that require no apology. Save your sorrys for when they are actually needed and they are genuine. Sorry when genuine and in the right context is strong. Continually apologising as a habit may show weakness and is disempowering. If you are a continual apologiser, try swapping out your 'sorrys' for more empowered words.

Feeling uncomfortable at times is part of the journey. I like to control feeling uncomfortable if I can, which I know is a strange thing to say. By that, I mean I need to push my comfort zone as often as I possibly can because I want that growth which is on the other side. I want to push my limits and see who I can become as a result of it. Staying in my comfort zone isn't an option and to me it isn't balanced. I need comfort, but I also need some challenge to grow as a person. At the moment public speaking makes me feel uncomfortable, so that's next on my list to really get good at. My focus right now is on overcoming the discomfort. I know I don't need to be the best speaker in the world; I just need to be comfortable and be myself whilst doing it and that is enough.

TRUTH BOMB: Feeling uncomfortable in the right context is proof that you are growing

On the same thread, we need to stop feeling guilty about things that we don't need to feel guilty about. So many of us are massive people-pleasers, or recovering people-pleasers, like me! If we don't want to do something, or if something isn't important to us, then we have the right to say no. We also have the right not to do it and not to feel guilty about it.

We waste so much time and energy on feeling guilty. I know I've wasted so much precious time on needless guilt. That time could be put to better use elsewhere. Usually we feel this way about things we don't need to feel guilty about. What if we just let it go? What if we just didn't automatically go into guilt mode and instead chose a better feeling?

It's not always that easy to let it go, but that is what we use our journals and reframing for. Drop the guilt where you can and keep your vibe high. Next time you feel needlessly guilty, bring it back to being grateful and focussed on the present moment. Use that energy for something positive instead.

Mindset Tool Summary

I want to summarise each mindset tool we have gone through as a refresher before we move on to Part Three. I am doing a summary, as the important thing is that you 'get' it and can see how it all fits into your life. Then you can start to think about how you can implement it.

Perspective

To me, perspective is deciding what matters most to you and choosing to put your focus there. It is choosing what is real to you and what actually matters to you, when all is said and done. Eventually when we are able to harness perspective, we keep it at the top of our minds. When we do that, so much that doesn't matter falls away. You let go of trivialities and will be able to see clearer, feel better and have more direction.

Think about what you need to put into perspective right now. Remind yourself to both use and keep perspective.

Reframing

The analogy of looking downstream helped me change the way I reacted to situations that arose. When I chose to look for the good over the bad, I had a much better experience all round. It allowed me to sidestep stress and feeling reactive, plus the knock-on effect that would have on my day. Use reframing when something doesn't go to plan or feels bad. Look at the situation in a way that feels easier and more comfortable to you. Flip it 180 degrees.

Next time something happens to which you would usually react negatively, reframe it and choose to focus on the good instead.

Gratitude

Hands down, gratitude is one of the most life-changing feelings we can have. For me, gratitude changed everything. This life-changing emotion enhances our lives, relationships, our capabilities, our outlook, and so much more. By coming from a place of gratitude, we can't help but lead a more enriching and fuller life. When we choose gratitude, we are choosing good for our body, mind and soul.

What can you be grateful for right now? Seriously, even when you feel like everything is falling apart, or you feel hard done by, there is always something you can be grateful for.

Meditation

Starting every day with a quiet mind has had a massive impact on me, and now I feel so much calmer and clearer. Quiet time to just clear my mind and start the day with a fresh slate has been so powerful. If you can feel yourself becoming overloaded, just stop for a few minutes and close your eyes. Sit still and focus on your breathing and enjoy it. Meditation has so many benefits and can change your state very quickly. Give yourself peace and a reset when you need it.

Close your eyes and take five-ten deep breaths. Then allow your breathing to normalise and just enjoy a few peaceful minutes.

Affirmations

We can bring what we want into being by using these powerful 'in the present' statements. By affirming what we want, we create new neural pathways in our brain. Remember, our brain can't tell the difference between what has happened or what we have imagined. Say it, think it, write it and believe it.

What can you start to affirm right now?

Visualisation

You are imagining what you want done, just like elite athletes do before a race. As with affirmations, you are creating new pathways in your brain to imagine what you want into existence. You can visualise anything you want, including how you want to be, something you want to achieve, or even being somewhere. What you can hold in your mind, you can bring into your life.

Try it out. Close your eyes and visualise the best version of you in tiny detail.

Intentions

Setting intentions in your journal about your day helps maximise achievement. Make your intentions a mix of things that will nourish your mind and body, and move the needle in your business. Don't be tempted to skip the self-care, which could include going to the gym, going for a walk, having a smoothie, reading a book for thirty minutes, or whatever makes you feel good. The only rule is that it should be just for you, away from everyday life. You can absolutely set intentions for your mood, your body, your life or whatever you want.

Start each day with setting intentions. Or even set an intention to be happy / calm / confident / etc. Set the intention, believe it and then make it happen!

Journaling

Journaling has helped me make sense of so much these past few years. Don't underestimate having private space and putting pen to paper. Journaling helps us understand our thoughts and feelings, situations and challenges. It helps us affirm our visions, design our lives, make decisions, get rid of blocks and false beliefs, overcome challenges and so much more. Use your journal to come to terms with decisions or realisations. Use it however you need.

You will never regret journaling. Make it a priority to try it out.

Remember all of this changed my life. I know if you stick to it, it can change yours too. We are going to be putting all the mindset strategies together and creating some action in Part Three.

I want to make a point about letting go of perfection. Balance is about being you, on your terms. It's doing the best you can with what you have and knowing it's enough. People love us for who we are; people want to see the imperfectly beautiful versions of us in all our uniqueness. I'm not perfect, you are not, no one is, so don't waste time worrying about it.

TRUTH BOMB: Don't be afraid of putting yourself out there, because you never know who needs to hear your message

Done is better than perfect in our lives, too. Whether it's our work tasks or something at home, done is better than perfect. Done doesn't mean second rate; done means the best with what we have and the time we have. Perfection doesn't exist and is unattainable. Doing our best is enough.

The Power of your Tribe

There are so many reasons why there is power in our tribes and why we all need a tribe to belong to. I have been so lucky throughout my journey to have the best group of women (and men) around me, who have helped me in so many ways. With the S&CBC, there's no doubt at all that I wouldn't be where I am without my tribe and I owe them all such a lot. Your tribe can be anyone you identify with – it could be your friends, a support network, being in a Facebook Group, anything.

Here are some of the benefits I see of having a support network or tribe, around you.

- Accountability
- Validation and sounding off ideas
- Development
- Learning

- Inspiration
- Self-care/wellbeing
- Ongoing support
- Business development
- Honest feedback
- Helping arrive at solutions
- Recommendations
- Boosting confidence and keeping you on track

We all need a support network. You might not have found yours yet but, as you grow, your energy is attracted to those just like you. People just like you will come into your world.

Accountability is at the top of the list as I believe this is so important. Whatever your goals are, having accountability can be transformational. I am in a business mastermind group, and every Monday we have a video call. I want to make sure I have achieved all I said I would achieve that week, so I don't let the rest of the team down. Equally we can have accountability in all sorts of areas, from weight loss to exercise, addiction and beyond. Don't underestimate the power of being held accountable.

There have been so many generous people who have supported me in one way or another on my journey. There are too many to mention, but they all know who they are and know I am grateful.

My darling Keiran and my family of course get a special mention for supporting me, believing in me and counselling me over the years. They have been through so much with me. Then there were my 'squad', my besties – Danielle, Sharon, Blowers, Sadler, Haley, Laura and Pip. Then there are literally tens of other women from my club who have supported me – from hosting events to just propping me up! I just want to take a moment to acknowledge them all, no matter how small their role has been.

They say we are the average of the five people we spend the most time with, so make sure you are with people who make you feel good and raise you higher. Surrounding yourself with people who inspire you can be difficult, but follow them online, go to in-person events, do what you can to get that valuable inspiration.

Don't hang around with people who bring you down.

In the same vein, I want to raise an important point about people. When you become this butterfly and evolve and grow, people will feel threatened. They will tell you you are wrong. Part of evolution and transformation comes with losing your old way of being. When you evolve, you will lose people, and that is ok. Your new, balanced life is going to cost you your old one, and that is more than ok.

On the flipside, you might inspire your tribe to up their game too. If you can do that and have an impact, then that is a real privilege. The important thing, though, is to remember that if you don't grow, you become a people pleaser. If you downplay your personality, which I did for years, you are giving away your power. You have a message and unique gifts and it is your duty to share them with the world.

It is about remembering to use all the tools and keeping the faith. I am looking forward to getting your business balanced in Part Three!

Action Step:

Let us know your takeaways from Part Two in the Facebook Group!

PART 3

THE SEVEN PRINCIPLES OF
BALANCE

For Business

I am delighted to introduce you to my 'Seven Principles of Balance'. I created the Principles out of necessity for balancing my own business. Many of my business coaching clients have successfully applied the Principles to their business and are yielding excellent results! The Seven Principles of Balance are effectively a framework which will enable you to become super-focussed and efficient – running the best possible version of your business – so you can lead the best possible version of your life.

Part 3 is action-based and walks you through the exact steps I took to get my business to a place of balance. I will go into more detail for each Principle and at the end there will be an action step for you. I can't wait for you to get stuck in to this section and to see what you can make happen in your business.

If you'd like to work with me directly on your business or business, visit www.victoriaknowleslacks.com to find out about my group and 1:1 coaching.

Principle One:

Mindset

"Progress is impossible without change; and those who cannot change their minds cannot change anything."
George Bernard Shaw

Mindset is the absolute foundation to getting your business balanced and working for you. So we can get our lives right! I genuinely believe that when you have the right mindset you can achieve anything. Positive momentum builds, doubts start to fall away and you begin to thrive. This is when you step into your power.

Principle One Outcomes:

- Understanding the key elements of a positive mindset
- Setting yourself up for success
- Implementing mindset tools
- Establishing habits

This Principle brings together the mindset tools we learned in Part Two and we are going to start introducing them into our daily lives, so we can form positive habits which will drive us forward. That's when the really good stuff starts to happen.

When we have positive habits, we ignite our potential and set ourselves up for the best possible chance of success. This is what we are aiming for. I have it and I am sharing all this with you so you can have it too.

Committing to my mindset practice has helped me form those positive habits in a sustainable and straightforward way. It's an addictive feeling – every single day I feel good. With this Principle it is my hope for you that, every single day, you are going to feel intentional, capable, grateful, aligned and striving towards your goals.

Principle One is a reminder that we must put ourselves front and centre and that we must make time for ourselves. We have to make ourselves a priority. It prompts us to remember our journey is a marathon, not a sprint. We must be strong, healthy and happy if we are going to go the distance.

TRUTH BOMB: Little, consistent shifts every day add up to big life changes

Element 1: Morning Routine

You know how my morning routine changed my life? Now it is time to get yours sorted. This will be the foundation for a more positive mindset and will become the catalyst for big change. By having time for yourself in the morning you may well find that you start to have better days, which lead to better months, which lead to better years and, before you know it, you are leading a much more fulfilled life. This was the case for me. Don't ever underestimate the power of having some quiet intentional time for yourself in the morning.

The myriad of benefits of a morning routine:

- Helps you reach your business and self-care goals through intentions
- Encourages optimism
- Fosters consistency
- Encourages positive physiological changes
- Allows you to stay aligned with your vision and goals

- Gives you focus to get through challenges in your journal
- Reminds you to utilise mindset tools
- Allows you to start the day in a positive space
- Over time the routine can expand
- Allows 'me time' that you can look forward to

Your life, commitments and schedule will determine the amount of time you can spend on your morning routine. Try it out for seven days and see what happens.

I understand that you are busy – you might have kids, a demanding job or something else which means you don't feel like you can make time. However I genuinely believe that you can make an extra ten minutes for yourself at some point in the morning. If you had to you would. Even if it's locking yourself in the bathroom or waking up before everyone else. I know you will experience the benefits of setting up your day. Make it happen and you will get the results.

If some days you can only do five minutes, and others you have twenty-five, go with what works for you. Be flexible with yourself, and know that something is better than nothing and your mindset should be a priority. When you are showing up for yourself, you show up better for others.

TRUTH BOMB: The best investment you can make is in yourself

I recommend you get yourself a beautiful notebook for this exercise. If you don't have one yet, there is a printable template for your daily success routine in your workbook to get you started.

My Morning Routine Format:

- Five minutes meditation.
- Three minutes visualisation.
- Setting Intentions (AM): Set three work-based intentions and three self-care intentions for the day.

- Gratitude: Write down five to ten things you are grateful for each day.
- Affirmations: Write three positive affirmations in the present tense.
- Journaling: Write how you feel, and challenge any blocks you might have. Reaffirm your vision or hopes and dreams.

This tried-and-tested formula has calmed the frantic side of my personality. It didn't transform me in an instant but, little by little, it brought about massive changes and pushed me to this point. Without doubt, my morning routine has been my secret weapon.

With this daily commitment and time to yourself, I have no doubt that you will transform too. Imagine how different things will be for you a year from now. As the months roll by and you stick to your practice, it will be great to look back on your journals. For me, it has been fascinating to see how far I have come. There is a massive change in my priorities, perspective and my thought processes. Sometimes we don't realise how much we're growing and changing, but we really are!

Movement is also a key part to a successful morning routine. Getting up and moving your body to get your energy going is of paramount importance. If you don't have time for a full workout, do what you can with what you've got. It could be twenty star jumps in the bathroom, jogging on the spot, or a good stretch in the kitchen! If you have the time to run, walk, or workout, then all the better. I walk in the mornings when it's not raining and I have some of my best ideas when I'm out wandering.

You may already have your own rituals you like to do in the morning. Add them in! The same goes with the evening. If you have ways to help you wind down, don't stop doing them. You can also extend the elements out longer so, for instance, you could do a twenty-minute meditation.

I am excited for you to start and to see how it changes your day, your week, month and year. You can build on this great foundation and bring in your own elements. Let us know in the Facebook

Group when you start your morning routine.

Tag me on Instagram @VictoriaKnowlesLacks with your photos too.

Element 2: Reframing

Reframing is a powerful habit. For me it became a life-changing one, suddenly I went from reactive to proactive, angry to understanding and was generally just more chilled out. You can save yourself a lot of bad feelings when you reframe those challenging situations. For me, it was as simple as flipping a difficult situation in my mind from not-so-good to something positive. This allowed me to prioritise inner peace and happiness, which has allowed my positivity to expand tenfold. To me, it is more important to be happy than to have the last word, get one over on someone, or be right. I got to this point from reframing and keeping perspective.

We need to keep reminding ourselves to look downstream and to see everything flowing better. The goal is to welcome as much ease as we can into our lives, and let what we don't want to flow away. When we do this our energy changes, we hold onto less negativity and we just feel more settled.

Note about reframing: This does not apply to massive trauma or deep-rooted experiences. With reframing, and in fact all of my mindset practices, it is about usual day-to-day situations.

I use reframing a lot and I have two main types of this practice to share with you:

1   The most popular reframe is the situational reframe. This is when you reframe things which happen which upset, surprise, hurt, provoke you or make you feel slightly uncomfortable. In really simple terms it's looking at the situation from a different perspective. If you need a refresher, turn back to Part Two.

2   The second type of reframing is the feeling reframe. It is when you take steps to start reframing your whole

outlook – little by little, step by step, day by day – which will positively impact on your life. Instead of defaulting to feelings of lack, defeatism or falling into victim mode, you reframe to remind yourself of how fortunate you actually are. From there, you are actively looking for good and positive momentum builds. Gratitude helps with this.

I want to challenge you to use a situation that you are dealing with right now, that is not 100 per cent comfortable. Write what it is at the top of a journal page, then come up with five more comfortable ways of looking at it.

As situations arise that need reframing, ask yourself the following questions:

- Will it matter in a month or a year from now? If not, can I just write it off?
- How is it going to feel if I react badly and what are the consequences?
- How is it going to feel if I respond positively and what are the consequences?
- What do I need to learn to move forward from this?
- Is the situation even meaningful to me? Is it something I care about or will it move me forward?

The more you reframe, the better you become at it; the better you become, the more you benefit and the happier you'll become. Try it and see how you get on. The key is to remember to reframe whenever you feel stress coming on, use phone reminders, have a post-it note on your desk, get accountability with a friend or family member. Do what you need to do to remember to reframe and get back on that good feeling!

TRUTH BOMB: Whatever happens, with your eyes on the prize, you can handle anything – you have to start telling yourself this! Commit to looking for another way and you will see it.

Element 3: Learning Lessons

In business, stressful events like a website crash or losing customers can teach us things. Make it a priority to take the lessons and move forward. Do what you need to do, take the stress for a few minutes if you need to, but then let it go and take the lessons.

We have to go through the bad stuff to be able to glean the gold – the lessons.

When something doesn't go your way, what can you learn? Remember, there is no such thing as failure and we must make mistakes to grow. I have made so many mistakes over the years and they were solid proof that I was trying. No one can ever judge you for trying.

TRUTH BOMB: No one who is doing more than you will run you down, only those who aren't will. Don't forget that.

Element 4: Confidence

I have learnt that we are infinitely capable and our potential is limitless, yet we choose to give into the voice in our heads. The dreaded lack of confidence is such a big deal for lots of us. Just like self-doubt, a lack of confidence can stop us from achieving the potential we were born for and that is a massive shame. Imagine if we just got on with things. What if we just put to one side all of those reasons we tell ourselves why we can't do something? Have a think about what is actually stopping you from just cracking on. I spent some time journaling this and I discovered that I had a fear of judgement, which probably came from being told off at school. Because I knew that and became aware of it, I could move it to one side and move forward in a more confident way. I know this isn't easy, but we must become aware of this voice (our ego) and start to challenge it. We weren't born to keep quiet and not share our message. Someone, somewhere needs to hear what we have to say.

You will have your own ways of growing in confidence. You might take massive action in pursuit of your goals, or use breathing techniques, you might visualise, or you might have a gin and tonic! Confidence is such a personal thing, but commit to growing yours and find ways to strive towards gaining more every single day. You have to get out of your comfort zone and get comfortable with feeling uncomfortable.

We must question what we are actually afraid of, then we must get to the bottom of it and question if it's more important than achieving what it is we want to achieve. It has taken me a while to make my motivation bigger than my ego, but I am getting there. I have become so much more confident, just by taking action and moving forward. Become your own source of validation; don't rely on others. Life is too short for you to be the only thing standing in your way.

TRUTH BOMB: Confidence often becomes courage and vice versa

On the subject of confidence, don't be afraid of showing your vulnerable side too. There is so much strength in vulnerability. Remember, other people don't know how you are feeling unless you tell them; so grow through your confidence, little by little. Can you remember the last time you didn't feel confident? Then, can you remember the last time someone else didn't feel confident? Exactly! We never know when someone lacks confidence, unless they let us know. Just own it!

Push yourself a little more every time. The rewards are always far greater than the risk.

The key to Principle One is getting yourself to a place of calm and knowing. It's about keeping the faith and having calm in your mind and approach. You are so much stronger than you know and you will overcome situations and challenges that present themselves. You will, because you must. When you know this, you become stronger.

Element 5: Establishing Positive Habits

So we know how to be more positive and we know what we need to do. We have to find a way to bring all of these elements into our lives every day, so that we can really experience and live the change. There is no 'one size fits all' approach to doing this – we need to find ways that work for us and that are sustainable. We are all different in the way we learn and implement habits, so it's up to you to find a way that works for you when you are living these mindset strategies every day.

Here's how I was able to create these positive habits:

- I committed 100 per cent to being more positive and changing my outlook. The motivation to me was leading a happier life, which was way more important to me than being right or being perfect.
- Committing to my morning routine without fail.
- Setting intentions to reframe / look for the good / see the lessons in my journal as part of my morning routine.
- Having accountability. Every time I would feel myself getting worked up or annoyed, my husband would remind me!
- Reducing as many triggers as I could which would bring on negative thoughts. I unfollowed a lot of social media accounts of people who I didn't align with. I removed myself from situations which didn't feel good and which I knew would make me reactive. I took a long, hard look at everything.
- Talking positively to myself brought on feelings of gratitude more and more, so it soon became the norm.

How can you establish positive habits? Like with all sustainable things, commit and take small steps every day in the direction you want to go. Do too much at once and you are setting yourself up for a fall. Get started, do what you can and see how your life unfolds.

Principle One Action points:

- Create your morning routine and commit to it. Let us know in the MAKE IT HAPPEN // MINDSET AND MOTIVATION // THE BOOK Facebook Group and Instagram using the hashtag #MakeItHappenBook. Start right now, do it every day and see what happens to your life and mindset.
- Create a plan to establish and implement positive habits, using reminders and prompts where necessary.
- Get accountability. Ask someone who can help you stay on track – a friend or family member, or find an accountability friend in the Facebook Group. Find someone you are comfortable with who can push you out of your comfort zone just a little bit more. We can always push a bit more.

Principle Two:

Clarity

"In absence of clearly-defined goals, we become strangely loyal to performing daily acts of trivia."
Author Unknown

The aim of Principle Two is to gain clarity as a starting point for a new way of running your business in a smarter and better feeling way. When we face up to what is going on and take our head out of the sand, we can finally begin to accept the reality of the situation. First acceptance, then change. My Clarity Plan was the catalyst for change for me and the point where my life started to turn around from that place of burnout. It is what brought me to sharing all this with you.

The aim of the Clarity Plan is to give you a high-level, yet simple, overview of everything that you do day-to-day in your business, so you can see where you are spending all your time – as opposed to where you actually should or should not be spending it. It is a great exercise to help you review, reflect and reorganise.

Principle Two Outcomes:

- Provoking thought to gain clarity
- Identifying all business functions
- Identifying where current focus is
- Valuing tasks to value time
- Inspiring thought of change

- Identifying inefficient systems

Having this clarity means we can take an objective and powerful look at where we are in our businesses. From there, we can start to build a picture of a new, more balanced way of operating. We also start to see where positive changes can be made, what we can cut back on and what we need to focus on more.

For me, clarity often accompanies big breakthroughs. By giving yourself the time and space to clear away some of the overwhelming feelings, or just clearing the mental clutter, that is when energy will be freed up for big change.

TRUTH BOMB: Clarity makes us productive and gives us the fire to succeed

All of the people succeeding in business know the importance of having clarity, as it energises us and pulls us forward.

No matter if you are running a brand-new start-up, or if you have been in business a while, I think it is so powerful to do this clarity exercise, and it is definitely worth the time it takes. Once you have done it, you will know exactly what you need to do less of. Often we are working 'in' our business and are bogged down with day-to-day tasks, instead of working 'on' our business and moving forwards with the higher-level strategy stuff. When I did that first Clarity Plan that I talked about in Part One, I can't tell you how great it made me feel to have that massive weight lifted from my shoulders.

Once we have a clear view of where we are, we'll be identifying the low-level tasks with a cost-per-hour associated value to see where we need to move our focus from or to. Trust me, this is such a liberating exercise.

I'm not sure about you, but I know that I held so many of my business processes and information in my head, which isn't conducive to balance at all – in fact, it's a recipe for burnout. We can't gain clarity if we have all of that information swirling around in our minds.

To me, there are two main reasons why we need clarity and why we need to get everything out of our heads and onto paper.

1   To stop you feeling overwhelmed. When everything is in your head, your energy and creativity tends to drop. You feel less capable, you feel stressed and everything feels like a massive uphill struggle.

2   To avoid limiting growth through lack of efficient systems and processes. If you mentally store large parts of how you do things, you limit your capacity to outsource. It's generally harder to scale when you do everything yourself.

Once you have completed your Clarity Plan, hold onto it, as we will refer to it in Principles Five and Six.

Ready? Let's begin. Turn to the Clarity page in your workbook.

Step 1: The Audit

In your workbook, list out all the tasks you perform in your business:

- Daily
- Weekly
- Monthly
- Annually
- Ad-hoc

First, list every single task or process that you complete, or is done for you, in your business. It's good to go into minute detail for this exercise, list everything you can think of. For some people, this will be really easy and you'll complete it quickly, but for others it's a lot more involved. If you are the latter, sleep on it or come back to it. It's an exercise where you can do it, walk away, come back and find there are nearly always more tasks that can be added. When I first did my audit I was shocked!

If you need to get your thoughts flowing, start with the spider diagram and then list the tasks under each heading. Really give thought to every single thing that keeps your business going, then think of some more!

Tip: If you are stuck, go through your calendar, email and Instagram for prompts. Still stuck? Spend a day or two logging every single thing you do in your planner and then come back to this exercise.

Below are tasks from my business, shared to spark thought and inspiration:

Daily Tasks: Emails. Responding to social media posts. Posting on social media. Checking all social platforms. Client check-in. Membership maintenance. Content writing. Admin. Showing up in your Facebook Group. Planning. Working on your goals (however that looks for you) and so on.

Weekly tasks: Planning and creating newsletters. Checking in with my team. Client calls. Creating graphics. Bookkeeping. Database management. Promotion. Scheduling web posts. Website updates. Uploading copy. Sending press releases. Invoicing. Creating weekly video. Weekly admin tasks. Member outreach. Facebook live planning. Facebook ads.

Monthly tasks: Guest blogging. Updating / improving website. Reviewing metrics and stats. Research. Q&A calls. Planning. Expenses. VAT returns. Content planning. Content recording. Social media planning. Blog planning. Expert / guest outreach. Affiliate support.

Annual / Ad Hoc tasks: Annual accounts. Website revamp. Annual goal setting. Course creation. Event planning.

Once you've done this, take some time to think about the systems you have in place. Use the space on your Clarity Plan to note what software, processes and tech you use, and rate it. We'll be looking at systems in Principle Five.

Step 2: The Value

Next we will attach a value to our time. I love to do this section as, for too long, I was so aimlessly busy – as you know. I kept burning out so much as I didn't have the focus I have now.

Putting an hourly value on all your tasks clearly identifies the low-value ones which are keeping you busy with little return, versus the ones where your focus needs to move to which have a higher return. It's also useful to see what low-value tasks we can release or outsource. This is such a powerful and impactful exercise for clarity and it's one of the favourites of the small business owners I coach!

In your Clarity Plan, go through each of the tasks you've written and give them either a value of £5, £50 or £500. You can add a £5000 price if you want to. We use £5 an hour tasks to illustrate low value. This doesn't mean that a social media helper or an admin person costs £5 per hour, but it easily identifies low value tasks. Energetically go with figures that work for you.

Below are some of the exact tasks which were in my last Clarity Plan in March 2018, which hopefully will help you identify which of your tasks have which value attached.

My £5 per hour tasks were:

- Scheduling social media posts (Twitter, Facebook and Instagram)
- Replying to posts on my business social media accounts
- Creating social posts from templates in Canva
- Uploading web copy and formatting posts
- Sending event emails
- Posting members badges
- Scheduling posts in my Facebook Group
- Replying to basic enquiries

My £50 per hour tasks were:

- Cleaning data records in the database
- Updating membership details
- Updating tech on my website
- Creating Facebook ads
- Bookkeeping / Accounting / Expenses
- Press outreach and PR
- Creating sign in lists for the events

My £500 per hour tasks were:

- Designing launches
- Designing opt-ins and lead magnets
- Creating paid member content
- Servicing my membership
- Planning
- Expert outreach

My £5,000 per hour tasks were:

- Dealing with sponsors
- Creating my online course
- Executing launches

There is no right or wrong answer to this – just go with what feels right for you. Once you have done this, take a moment to appreciate and acknowledge yourself and how far you have come. Chances are you have been doing so much for so long to get here. Take a few moments to breathe it all in and to feel proud.

TRUTH BOMB: You will benefit exponentially when you take time to clear the decks and get real with yourself and where you are

How do you feel after doing this exercise? You might feel surprised about the amount you've been doing, or maybe you've realised your focus has been in totally the wrong place for a long time. Maybe you are focusing on chasing the money, but you don't have a handle on your admin? Maybe your priorities are all wrong and you realise that your revenue-driving tasks are too far down your list?

For me, doing my first Clarity Plan was profound. I was absolutely ready for change and I was ready to do the work; and because of that I could clearly see where I was going wrong. The Clarity Plan showed me what I was doing was low-level and unproductive – it highlighted all my 'busy' work.

Now that you have a clear picture, think about these questions for now:

- What can you change easily?
- What can be automated, streamlined or delegated?
- Which long-winded processes can be simplified?
- Which technology or software would massively help you?
- What can be removed from your task list altogether?
- Have you had any inspiration or 'a-ha' moments or changes you can make?

We will return to the Clarity Plan in Principle Five and Six where we'll look at automation, streamlining and outsourcing. Before then, if anything profound springs to mind or if you have any flashes of inspiration, make a note of them. It is exercises like these that spark thoughts which inspire us and help us see the way ahead.

If you feel overwhelmed by doing this exercise and feel like you need some support or inspiration, reach out in the Facebook Group, or start flexing your reframing muscle! Even though you might be feeling a bit like it's all too much, that is actually a really good thing and it's a sign that you are pushing yourself – you are growing!

I hope you will feel more optimistic once you've been through this exercise. This is as deep as it gets. If you want to, you can write a few notes about how you feel in your journal and capture the feeling. Note any emotions that arise, whether it's optimism, excitement, or hopefully, clarity. Take it one step further and close your eyes for a few minutes to start visualising what your business will look like once you've implemented the changes. Then, when you are ready, we will get started with Principle Three.

Action Step:

Complete your Clarity Plan and share any breakthroughs or takeaways in the **MAKE IT HAPPEN // MINDSET AND MOTIVATION // THE BOOK** Facebook Group, or tag me on Instagram @VictoriaKnowlesLacks and use the hashtag #MakeItHappenBook.

Reward yourself with something for facing up to this challenge and getting it done! It's actually a really big thing to go this deep on where you are with your business and not burying your head in the sand. We're going to build on this in Principle Three and create your big, amazing vision.

Principle Three:

Vision

"The secret of getting ahead is getting started. The secret of getting started is breaking your complex overwhelming tasks into small manageable tasks and then starting on the first one."
   Mark Twain.

Principle Three is my favourite as it's about defining what we actually want for our businesses and how we are going to make it happen. We are going to start making our vision a reality with microsteps for big impact. It's all about putting one foot in front of the other and getting going.

Principle Three Outcomes:

- Creating your big business vision
- Defining your Biggest Impact Goals (BIG's)
- Creating your Forward Action Step Tasks (FAST's)
- The Reality and Reward (RAR)
- Bringing it into your day-to-day life

This Principle is broken down into two key parts:

- Creating your vision
- Identifying the ways to achieve it

TRUTH BOMB: Imagine what your business will be like a year or two years from now if you get started today?

The key to creating your first vision is to just get started and put pen to paper. Don't judge your thoughts or talk yourself out of anything before you've even got going. Don't reject things based on your beliefs about yourself. Go with what lights you up, feels good and excites you.

Tip: Imagine someone could grant a wish and give you the business you want? This is the kind of vision we want. Define it – don't talk yourself out of it – then you can make a plan to get there.

Turn to the Vision page of your workbook. This is where we're going to let the thoughts flow. If you don't have a business yet, that's fine. The more details we can log here, the better. Give yourself some time for this and enjoy the process. There's something so exciting about writing your future story and creating your vision.

Stage 1: Creating your BIG vision for your business

Answer the questions below in as much detail as you can and as though you already have what you want. Writing as though you already have what you want is really powerful.

For now, leave the 'Goal' line underneath your answers blank. You can pick out the goals once you have answered the questions.

- What does your future business do and how does it look like for you? For example, is it a membership site, product-based, online course, or coaching? Write in as much detail as possible.
- What sets you apart from other businesses? Why do clients love you so much? What is it about you and your business that people love?
- How are you growing your audience? How are you making it easy for your ideal client / student / members / subscribers / customers to find you? List three things you can do to grow your audience.

- How are you serving your audience and offering big value? List three ways in which you can do this.
- What impact do you make? Big or small, we all make an impact. How can you make more of an impact on people and the world?
- How much revenue are you bringing into the business and are there multiple revenue streams? Where is the money coming from?
- What are the next steps for your business? What new products or services will you be introducing?
- What systems do you have in place to make your business run like clockwork? Think about how it all looks.
- Do a SWOT analysis (Strengths, Weaknesses, Opportunities, Threats) of your business. It's important to put your full thought to each category and brainstorm it, so you have a balanced overview. Strengths and Opportunities often come easier to list, whereas Weaknesses and Threats often takes more thought. Include any obstacles that you might have. What are the possible risks to your business, whether it's a gap in skills or threats to your industry, competition and so forth?

Once you have your answers, sit with them for a while and acknowledge this amazing feeling. You can make this possible. All you have to do is to commit, work out the details and do the work, which I know from experience is entirely possible.

Next, we're going to make a note of any obvious goals, with each of your answers on your goal line. Note that not every answer will have a goal.

Here's an example of how we do it:

If your answer to Question 1 was to have an online course teaching women to be more confident, your goal is to '*Create an Online*

Course'. Then, we're going to use those goals in the next step.

Question 2 – *"Why do your customers love you?"* – might or might not be a goal, depending on your answer. You might already be doing whatever it is they love. If you are not, then that's a goal and it needs defining. Let's use the example of *"An amazing customer experience"* – that's your goal that needs defining.

Stage 2: Defining Your Biggest Impact Goals (BIGs)

Stage 2 is about making a plan to get your vision into reality. At this point I want to remind you that you don't need to have every single tiny detail worked out, nor do you need to stick to this to the letter. Things will evolve as you get started, so keep flexibility in mind. You do need a strong vision and a plan to get started though!

Let me introduce you to 'BIGs', or Biggest Impact Goals. These are the big, chunky goals, we will define and prioritise to achieve in the next three to six months.

From Stage 1 choose the goals that are going to have the biggest impact.

For me, and for writing this book, my BIGs were:

Growing and serving my audience

As I'm starting from scratch with a new audience, I identified building my email list as my first BIG. I needed to identify ways to help my audience resonate with me, how to convey that and get them to sign up to my email list. From there I could offer meaningful and useful content, build a deeper relationship with them and serve them more. I decided Instagram stories would be the best fit for me as I could be the best, most authentic version of myself via video, offer value to people and ask them to opt-in to my email list if they wanted to. I created a personal website with free downloadable resources, in return for the downloaders' email addresses. I created a Facebook page for myself, with my email opt-in page on.

Creating a Community

My BIG is to create a framework and community that will resonate and have a positive impact on entrepreneurs who are ready to make it happen, and go after what they want, in a balanced way. The community would be a place where I can show up to serve, and where others can support each other too. I know the power of bringing together like-minded people.

To launch this book

To create a launch plan and strategy to get this book out into the world, including a launch team, joint venture partners, press and publicity etc.

These are just a few of my BIGs. In your workbook, complete the exercise and drill down on what your BIGs are. You can go into more detail if you like – do what aligns with you.

Stage 3: Creating your Forward Action Step Tasks (FASTs)

Stage 3 goes from goals to tasks, and from big to bite-sized. This is the 'nitty-gritty' of what needs to be done in order to achieve what you want. This is where you break it down further so you can start work.

Let me tell you about 'FASTs', or forward action step tasks. FASTs are the small, but vital, tasks within each BIG, that move us towards those goals – baby steps that move the needle. Chances are you might have tens of FASTs per goal and that's okay. The more we have the easier it's going to be for us. FASTs are our roadmap to what we want. They give us that all important clarity and enable us to identify what we can delegate or what we can streamline.

Here's how that is done:

Turn to the BIG page of your workbook. Write your BIG at the top and list every single action you need to take to make it happen.

We're going into minute detail here – all of the teeny-tiny steps we need to take to make it happen.

There will be things on your list which you won't have the necessary experience for – such as tech installs. Instead of learning it, you will probably be better off outsourcing it. Keep this in mind and start to think about the £5 an hour tasks too. We will talk about outsourcing in Principle Six.

When you are ready, start writing whatever comes in your head. As with the Clarity Plan in Principle Two, don't judge it – just let it flow and see what you come up with.

Here are examples of my FASTs which will get me to my BIG of growing my audience:

- Brainstorm opt-in freebie.
- List 5 ideas of valuable printables or resources that my potential audience will find useful.
- Ask my Instagram audience which two or three they would prefer, using online polls.
- Design winning lead magnets.
- Create a landing page on my website where people opt-in and receive the lead magnet.
- Set up a Mailchimp account to store my lovely new subscribers.
- Brainstorm an email nurture sequence to give value and to let subscribers know more about me and offer value.
- Pinpoint what value the subscriber will get from being on my list and write the emails.
- Set up email sequence in Automation.
- Draft text and source appropriate pictures for three different Instagram and Facebook ads. With the goal of taking people to my opt-in page to encourage them to sign up for my free resource.
- Research audience pain points and brainstorm a webinar around it.

- Design webinar and promote via Facebook and Instagram ads to collect emails.
- Offer massive free value on the webinar.
- Add call to actions to all my blogs.
- Plan useful Instagram and Facebook content with a call to action.
- Investigate pop-ups to capture email addresses on my website (apps like SumoMe) etc.
- Guest blogs with links back to my site. Offering value to someone else's audience and mention a valuable resource on my website where people can subscribe. Write a list of potential, relevant websites I can reach out to.
- Brainstorm a three-part video series offering to help solve a problem for my audience and promote it via Facebook ads.
- Plan and curate beautiful Instagram posts which resonate with people, offer value and have a call to action.
- Podcasts: Identify a list of podcasts I'd love to be featured on, where I can go on and offer value, and share a resource. Reach out to my list once it's done.
- Create a contest where people can win a copy of my book in return for their email address.
- Continue to add massive value on my podcast and bring in guests who will resonate and help my listeners.

As you can see, I have a really clear picture now of what I need to do to grow my audience. Within that list there will be FASTs that I can break down further but, importantly, I have captured all the things I need to do to get me started and it takes the pressure off me trying to remember it all! The more mental bandwidth we can give ourselves the better, as we free up space to focus on the things we want.

So, back to my FAST list, it all needs prioritising and storing somewhere I can access easily and tick things off. I love to use As-ana, but sometimes I use Google Sheets or Wunderlist, or there have been times when I print off my latest list and have it on my desk. This helps me stay aligned with my goals and I love to physi-cally tick things off when I've completed them.

When you have your FASTs list, you can prioritise and start al-locating time to each step. Your FAST list will evolve as things change, but that's ok; just update it as you go. Every Sunday I plan my week using my FAST list to ensure I am as productive as I can be, I call this my 'Sunday Session' and I spend around fifteen min-utes with my planner, preparing for the week ahead. The feeling of getting on top of Monday before it arrives is great.

Then on a daily basis I'll set my intentions from my FAST list. It's so easy to just pick the tasks out and get on with them. By working in this way it allows me to be really intentional and get all of the things I need to get done which take me towards my goals, but I don't have all the brain fog or procrastination around it be-cause I've spent the time doing this.

I balance my workload and set my hourly time blocks. I pick the FAST to start each day that will have the biggest impact on my goals, and work down from there. Also on a Sunday, I review the previous week. I look back on challenges, check into see if I took care of myself enough, what my energy was like and what I got done. This is something that really illustrates where I need to up my game or shine some light.

Use your affirmations to visualise completing each task with ease. Aim to complete at least one, if not more of your FASTs a day. Even when there are hard days and you don't have time, pick the quick wins and the ones which will take you the least amount of time. The idea is to feel like you are moving forward.

Just a note about how it all looks. When you do your FAST list you might feel a little bit overwhelmed and it all might seem a bit too much. Let me assure you, though, that this isn't just a ton of work to do – this is your pathway to success and balance. This is your amazing, bright and balanced new future. Your roadmap to taking it one step at a time and knowing exactly what needs to be done! It you do feel a bit overwhelmed, this is the perfect moment to look downstream.

Stage 4: The Reality and Reward (RAR)

Stage 4 is the reality check and self-care aspect. When you start working on your FASTs, you will be getting a lot done in a short amount of time. However, this book is all about balance so do not overload yourself. Baby steps, remember.

Creating your BIGs and FASTs sounds easy and lovely in theory. Using them is a tried and tested method that has yielded big results for a lot of the small business owners I work with. However, as with anything, there will be tough times, especially as you are growing. Acknowledge that it isn't easy. Be kind to yourself.

There will be things on your FAST list that you don't want to do, and you will somehow come up with the most elaborate excuses why you can't do them. You can do them, but it's also important to cut yourself some slack when you feel you need it. Be honest with yourself. There's a difference between taking some time out for rest and deliberately avoiding something. Revisit your mindset tools and reward yourself for coming so far. Journal, meditate, affirm your worth and your goals. This is your space to get to the bottom of what's stopping you. Seek the solution for yourself.

TRUTH BOMB: You didn't come this far to only come this far. There is a beauty to the strength that comes from tough times

This is where I want to introduce you to RARs (Reality and Reward). A RAR is an incentive for when the going gets tough and you need some encouragement. There will be items on your FAST list that you will procrastinate on in a big way, and there will be tasks that you are dreading.

When you are faced with uncomfortable situations in business, you first need to change your perspective. Then, incentivise yourself. Incentives, or rewards for getting through situations, have really motivated me these past few years. It's amazing how you can push through the impossible, or how quick you can get something done when you dangle yourself a carrot! Incentives are such a nice way of bargaining with yourself, and being kind to yourself, at the same time.

Not every reward needs to cost money and I regularly set myself incentives for ones that don't. Sometimes I might reward myself with an early finish, a long hot bath, some quiet time in the steam room at the gym, a picnic in the summer, a lie-in, a laptop-free afternoon. You get the idea!

Your action for Stage 4 is to pick out the RAR tasks where you know you will feel resistance. Journal through what you can in terms of any blocks you can foresee – anything that feels a bit icky – then set yourself a reward for when you do it.

Let us know in the MAKE IT HAPPEN // MOTIVATION AND MINDSET // THE BOOK Facebook Group or let me know on Instagram @VictoriaKnowlesLacks what your RARs are. You just never know who can help with them, or who can offer perspective.

I have a few more questions about you and your vision for you to answer in your workbook, before we move onto Principle Four

- What's your WHY for the business? Why are you doing it? When you connect with this it's so powerful.
- What work do you focus on in the business? Aside from being the face of your company, what work are you doing day-to-day?
- Where do you have help? (Do you have a team or use freelancers? What help is in place and what are they doing?)
- How do you feel every day? How do you hold yourself? How are you treating people? What message does your body language send?
- What will your ideal day look like? How many hours a day do you work?

- What have you had to learn to take your business to this new level? (To be more confident? To get over your fear of Facebook Live or public speaking?)
- What have you had to let go of? What old beliefs have you had to work through to enable you to move forward? Journal these out.
- How many days holiday do you give yourself? When are you not working? What are your boundaries?
- How are you feeling when you are not working?

Answer these questions and get an idea of how you are going to feel in this new, more organised and balanced space. You absolutely can do this. I know you can and I know you deserve all of the balance and clarity that is coming your way. There will be RARs that scare the hell out of you, but you need to make your dreams bigger than your fears, and don't forget those incentives!

TRUTH BOMB: If it was super easy, it wouldn't be worth having or doing. The strength comes from the journey

Stepping up in your business and dialling down the stress doesn't happen instantly, but know that through your daily mindset practice and by gaining all of the precious clarity from these Principles, you will get there.

It is important that you are realistic in what you can achieve every week. Don't overload yourself. Take big action, but take care of yourself too. Remember, leeway is a big part of balance and it's ok not to be organised all the time. Just get back up and on it when you can.

Bring your FASTs into your Daily Success Routine. Every day, in your 'intentions' section, list what you are going to achieve that day. You may even prefer to write them into your gratitude section when you've completed them. Celebrate every FAST achieved and celebrate every other win from that day.

How good does it feel to work through all of this? Having clarity is a real luxury for so many people, as they just never have it.

With the right mindset and clarity, you will become unstoppable. It really isn't that hard – we just make it hard.

You deserve all the success that's coming your way. Don't push it away; instead, pull it towards you. Visualise how it feels and use your affirmations. Take the steps you've listed in your FAST list and do the mindset work. Commit and you will achieve. With all the success and this clear workload, you are going to need the right boundaries in place.

If you want to share your big goals, tag me on Instagram @VictoriaKnowlesLacks, use the hashtag #MakeItHappenBook.

BONUS Exercise: As our ambitions and expectations grow, we must grow too. New ways require new beliefs and a fresh approach. Work on things in your journal or affirm and visualise who you need to become.

Principle Four:

Boundaries

"When we fail to set boundaries and hold people accountable, we feel used and mistreated."
Brene Brown

Every single day I want to feel empowered, unstoppable and creative. I want to be the best possible version of myself. In order to do this I need to be well rested, well nourished and I need to have boundaries in place, so I know where the line is and so do people around me. Being available 24/7 is mentally and physically exhausting and unnecessary. It may be acceptable for a short period in exceptional circumstances but, for prolonged periods, it is just a recipe for burnout.

Principle Four is about identifying and creating boundaries and space around you. It's about drawing a line in the sand between you, people and your business. It's about setting out expectations with others so you can protect your time, wellbeing and energy, in order to start to live your best life.

TRUTH BOMB: Having boundaries does not make you selfish

Principle Four Outcomes:

- Understanding why we need boundaries
- A look at where you can implement boundaries
- Protecting your time and energy

- Creating a boundary plan
- Implementing boundaries

Generally speaking, people will treat you how you treat yourself, so if you demonstrate respect of your time and space, others should respect it too. We need to educate people around us on what's acceptable and let them know what they can expect from us. People actually function better when they know where they stand and, by communicating or demonstrating your boundaries, you are saving them guesswork – so everyone is happy!

TRUTH BOMB: Your time and energy are the most precious things you have

I have highlighted four key areas where I have needed to form and incorporate boundaries. They form the basis of this Principle and have helped to transform my life.

They are:

- Time
- Communication
- Personal
- Other

Time

It's not just other people we need to set time boundaries with, we also need to set them with ourselves. Time boundaries are the ones related to how we spend our time, and include stopping us from feeling the need to work all of the time (and not feeling guilty about it). Giving ourselves the gift of time and space is one of the kindest things we can do for ourselves.

I now work six hours a day, which might sound luxurious and indulgent, but I am actually more productive in this well-planned and organised time than I was working a fourteen hour day doing things that were not focussed or productive. Having a working hours boundary of six hour days has made me become super-productive, and I work in a very focussed way now. I actually feel like I am thriving. I have a lot to look forward to outside of work, instead of cancelling plans for the sake of work like I used to. The knock-on effect has been massive, including being far more active, healthy, enthusiastic and just generally feeling better. Having this time boundary has also eradicated potential guilt or hang-ups for not working non-stop.

I have other boundaries for my own time too, which include meetings, work-related travel, and other people's expectations. Now I only say yes to things that are really important, because to me nothing is more important than my time and energy – both are abso-lutely vital to my happiness and health.

Communication

On the one hand, it is incredible how social media connects us but, on the other, for so much of the time we are way too available. This can be exhausting and overwhelming. We need to strike a balance with communication boundaries, and this is without even touching on the comparisons we can make with people on social media – and how that can make us feel!

If your community or audience are mainly online, it is really important that you lay out to others what is acceptable and what is not, in terms of how people contact you and when they can expect a response. In my business, I had to start setting expectations of when people could expect a response from me – otherwise I felt guilty – and it was just getting out of hand. I had to tell my audience that I wasn't always available and what my office hours were. It was a slightly uncomfortable prospect, but I knew that the reward was greater than that feeling and that it had to be done. I took email off my phone as it was becoming intrusive, so I put an auto-responder on my email which spelled out that people could expect a reply within two business days. I asked my audience to kindly not ask me work-related questions via Facebook Messenger, but to email me instead, which was well received and felt wonderful. I took my phone number off my website and explained that I would only reply to emails. It all worked out well and people respected it. When you are clear and polite, people don't mind at all.

Having communication boundaries means you can put your phone down and step away from your laptop. People don't expect a reply straight away, so don't disrupt special family time or drop what you are doing to reply to an email on a Saturday night – when the sender isn't even expecting a reply until Monday anyway! Communication boundaries give you peace of mind and space, and they allow you to be present in what you are doing.

Personal

So, once a buffer between you and work is in place, and you are clear when and how people should contact you, it is then time to ring fence your personal time with boundaries.

When we are talking personal boundaries, we are talking about saying no to what you don't want to do; we are talking losing obligations, and not being roped into things you don't want to do.

TRUTH BOMB: You don't have to say yes to everything

You don't have to answer the phone every time a friend calls with gossip. You don't have to go out with the people you don't want to go out with. You don't have to go to the tenth family party in a row. To feel better, you have to let go of as much unnecessary obligation as possible. If you are used to putting other people and what they want before you, then you need to change it up, politely and firmly, and do what you want to do.

Start saying "no" more

Personal boundaries cover self-care too. Make time every single day for "you" and don't let people encroach on it. It could just be your morning routine, or you might have non-negotiable time for a yoga or gym class. Whatever it is, just be clear with people. You need time for you in order to replenish your energy, and to be the best version of you.

Not being ruled by your phone is a great personal boundary. Do a screen-free challenge – leave it in another room for an hour or two, or push yourself further and go out without it! Or if you feel you need it in case of an emergency, take it with you, but turn it off and pack it away somewhere safe. Leave it in the car when you see your family. When you get off your phone and into the present, you will experience so much good.

Other

I have a few 'other' boundaries too, these are smaller, but still hugely important boundaries. The "other" category sweeps up everything else, and includes not working with people who don't give me a good vibe, or who I don't align with. If people or companies feel difficult, or if they just don't feel right, then I don't work with them. For me it is just not worth it. I have got rid of business relationships which felt forced, or which had become one-sided, and it felt very liberating. Similarly, choosing not to work with clients who don't feel like a good fit is a great boundary..

TRUTH BOMB: You absolutely can work less and achieve more

Creating your boundary plan

Hopefully by now you have some ideas of boundaries that you can put into place. Refer back to your workbook and turn to your boundary page and we're going to create a boundary plan.

On its own, even the act of identifying where we need boundaries can make us feel lighter and, just knowing we are going to put them in place, can make us feel so much less burdened.

It is important to remember why we are setting boundaries, so we can easily stick to them. For me it was about getting my life back, losing guilt, doing business (and life) on my terms and just having space around myself. As a result, they have enabled me to do my best work, make the biggest impact and run a business that fits around my life.

Note: This exercise is just for you; no one else is going to see it, so be brutally honest!

Step 1: Identifying where we need boundaries

So you know my boundaries and how I put them in place. Now it's time to start identifying where you need yours. Using the bullet points below, take some time to go through which boundaries are relevant to you. If you can think of any other areas where you need them, make a note, highlight them in your workbook and we'll create our plan to get them in place in Step 2.

Time Boundaries:

- Set realistic working hours that suit you. With your FAST lists, you will be upping your efficiency, so you can reduce your hours.
- Can you do meetings via video to save you time, cost and energy?
- Let clients know what is acceptable to you and when they can contact you (if you are a coach, service provider etc). Do you need a document to lay out expectations etc?
- Be selective on projects with tight deadlines.
- Identify time wasters and time sucking people; and restrict their time and access to you.

Communication Boundaries:

- Does everyone have access to you all the time? Do you need to address anything here?

- How do you handle your email? Does it need to change?
- How and when do you respond to messages on social media? Are you on it all the time?
- Phone time – do you take calls in your business? If so, during what hours?
- If you have a team, do they know when it's acceptable to contact you?

Personal:

- Self-care time – where can you add some non-negotiable 'You' time'?
- Holidays – book them into your calendar. Even if you can't go away, you can get away from your screen.
- Make your bedroom a phone-free zone – can you commit to this? Read in bed instead of scrolling!
- Look to wean yourself off social media or drastically cut down your phone time. Put the focus on you and looking after you, not strangers on the Internet.
- Leave business out of your relationship. Make your 'You' time about you and the ones you love.
- What can you let go of, especially where you currently feel obliged to do things that don't align with you?
- How about people speaking to you in a certain way (belittling or running you down). What action can you take?

Other:

- Saying no to working with people when you don't feel aligned with them.
- Saying no to invitations and events that don't align with your agenda or if you don't want to attend!

- Not working with people with inflated egos, their own agendas, or general bad vibes around them.

Hopefully there are a few items which resonate with you from the list above, and that you will feel confident to implement. How many potential boundaries you have will depend on your business and personal preferences. There is no right or wrong way of doing this. The thing with boundaries is that they are there to make our lives easier. Don't overthink it – just put them in place.

Pick five boundaries from your list that you can implement today. Those boundaries should make your feel empowered, inspired and clear some space around you.

Step 2: Creating and setting your boundaries

Once we have our five, or more if you wanted to list more, we will devise an easy way to put them in place, with the necessary action required. Just like with our FASTs, we need to break things right down, so they are easier to make happen.

I want to share an example from my Boundary Plan with you. There are just two points. Start with five of your own and, if you want to push ahead and do more, by all means do. Some of the small business owners I have worked with have really gone to town with this exercise, and have what I call a 'Boundary Blitz' – where they spend a week or so restructuring their entire business with new boundaries!

An example from my Boundary Plan:

Set working hours: I wanted to set working hours I could stick to, so I could take back a lot of my time.

Boundary: Working six hours a day from 9am – 3pm.

Action: Journal out any resistance or feelings of guilt I have around working less, as this was quite a change. Inform people what I'm doing to manage expectations. Put my new hours on my website, email signature and other communications. Create an autoresponder stating new hours and when customers can expect a reply. Start every day with a very clear plan and time block all of my FASTs. Book something in the diary for 3:30pm, so I have to down tools and leave. Set a reminder at 2pm to do the last push, so I don't work over.

Handling email: Not spending all day in my inbox or letting email take over my downtime.

Boundary: Check email twice a day only.

Action: Take email off my phone, as it felt intrusive and some emails affected my day and mood. Plus I was checking it at all times of the day and night! Set up a permanent email auto-responder to tell people when to expect a response and auto directing them to where they can book events. Do at least one FAST before I check my email around 10am. Have one final check around 2:30pm. Communicate this new way of email to my audience to manage expectations.

They are just two game changing, but easy to implement boundaries I put in place which genuinely changed things for me.

In your workbook create your list of boundaries and the steps you need to take. If there are any smaller quick wins while you are doing it, add them too – things like asking people not to contact you about work via Messenger etc. Always make sure you communicate your boundaries politely, have support in place like an auto responder, or some kind of expectation laid out for your audience, and stick to them. Sometimes you will need to exercise a bit of flexibility, but just make sure you are sticking to them 99 per cent of the time.

TRUTH BOMB: When you take control of your time, your life starts to change in positive ways

There might be some boundaries which aren't appropriate to implement right now and that's ok. Go with what feels right for now and make a note for a few months down the line.

For me, once I had implemented my first few initial boundaries, I could start to see all the other places where I needed them. I really started to respect my own time more and that had a great impact on how I felt about myself. I no longer felt beholden to anyone. As you evolve further you will spot more areas where you need more boundaries.

Let us know what your boundaries are in the Facebook Group – MAKE IT HAPPEN // MINDSET AND MOTIVATION // THE BOOK. What your before and after looks like with your boundaries. Also, if you need some support or inspiration, let us know.

Principle Four aims to give you your power back. It enables control, space and doing things in a way that suits you. In turn, you feel more calm, empowered and balanced.

Principle Five:
Streamlining and Automation

"Time = Life, therefore, waste your time and waste your life, or master your time and master your life."
Alan Lakein.

The big guns, streamlining and automation, are at the core of a balanced business. This Principle is all about making your business as time-efficient as possible, so you can work less and live more. We're going to be deep-diving into putting tasks and processes on autopilot, so you can step out of parts of your business.

Principle Five Outcomes:

- Understanding what are streamlining and automation
- Streamlining your time and how to work efficiently
- Streamlining your business processes
- The S&A (streamline & automation) Audit

What are streamlining and automation?

To me, these two balance powerhouses go hand-in-hand. To streamline means to simplify, and to automate is to put on to autopilot. Who doesn't want a simplified business with as much of it as possible on autopilot?

When we streamline, we are looking to do things smarter and in an easier way, whilst getting the same results – or better. It's looking for ways that allow us to step out of working 'in' our business, so we can work 'on' our business. When we are working 'on' our business, this is where we make big steps forward.

Automation is about identifying areas where you replace your time with systems and processes, so you stop working so hands-on. You can automate so many different areas including email list building, sales, customer on-boarding, scheduling and many more. It's a real game changer!

What are the benefits?

When we are streamlined, we are more efficient, less stressed, and we save time and energy for ourselves to live our lives. We are taking away the busy work.

Principle Five is broken down into two key areas:

- Streamlining your time and how you work. This applies to your day-to-day, and involves creating a balanced and streamlined way of working going forwards.
- Streamlining your business. Making it as easy as possible for you.

We are going to look at streamlining your time first and give you a strategy of how to work smarter and not harder.

Element 1: Streamlining your time

In this element, we are going to be looking at:

- Why you must stop multitasking
- Parkinson's Law
- Time blocking
- Batch working

You've got to stop multitasking...and here's why

From a recently retired, lifelong multitasker, I now know that in order to get the best results and to do our best work, we have to focus on one thing at a time. This may sound scary or unrealistic to you – it did to me – but I guarantee this will help you increase your output and standard of work. I have some very sound reasons why for you:

Research done by the University of London showed that people who multitask see a big drop in their IQ. This drop is sometimes up to fifteen points, which puts multitaskers on the same mental wavelength as people who have missed a night's sleep.

University of Sussex neuroscientists Kep Kee Loh and Dr Ryota Kanai also did a study in this area. Their findings showed people who frequently use more than one device have less grey matter in the brain. Their research supports earlier studies, showing connections between high media multitasking activity and poor attention in the face of distractions. This is along with emotional problems, such as depression and anxiety.

Multitasking tends to lower the quality of your work as you are not focussed. When we multitask, we often feel rushed which can lead to anxiety. It is just not a streamlined way of working, trying to do ten things at once. By bringing in our FASTs and focussing on one thing at a time, we work in a smarter, calmer and more efficient way.

Are you willing to give it a go? I highly recommend you do.

Have you heard of Parkinson's Law?

I want to introduce you to Parkinson's Law which has been so useful for me. For those who are not familiar, this law was created by Cyril Heathcote Parkinson in the 1950s. The Principle explains that "work expands to fill the time available for its completion". So, if you give yourself a week to do a blog post, it will take you a week; if you give yourself thirty minutes, it will only take thirty minutes. Keep this in mind when working on projects and managing the time you put aside for things. Also keep it in mind for the things on your list that you keep kicking back and not doing.

Block and Roll!

Blocking my time – combined with my FASTs – pushed me forward like you wouldn't believe! This exceptional and powerful combination have supercharged the way I work. Bold statement I know, but spending time to get organised and stay focussed with this productivity duo have changed everything. This is why I am getting so much done and working less.

My working day now consists of one-hour blocks or 'sprints'. I work in these blocks with Parkinson's Law in mind, and that bit of time pressure is great. I want things ticked off my list, as it makes me feel like I am really accomplishing something.

Here's how I block my time

- Have my list of FASTs for the day ready for when I start work. Having a daily plan is crucial
- Set the timer on my phone for an hour
- Work on that day's FAST only. Don't get distracted by email or social media in that hour
- When the time goes off, get up and move
- If the task wasn't finished, schedule it for another block, or move on to the next FAST

TRUTH BOMB: The power in time blocking is giving your brain a rest and moving your body

Batch working

Batch working is a brilliant way to streamline your time and it works beautifully with time blocking. You are effectively allocating time to do one thing repeatedly and creating a stockpile of work in a certain area. To work like this takes the pressure off you in a big way, especially if you are ill or something crops up; you then have a bank of content or whatever it is to work with. Being on a content treadmill every week is stressful, as is putting out substandard work because you've run out of content. I've been there – it's not cool, but batching really helps with this.

Focus on one area at a time and create your stockpile of things – such as creating blogs, podcasts, Instagram captions, videos and newsletters. When you are in that focussed, creative space, keep going and, instead of doing one, do many!

I have four days every month when I batch create content, re-gardless of what it is. I'll spend two days outlining and brainstorm-ing, two days creating, recording, writing or promoting etc.

Batch working has been key to having a business that fits around me, because I have my content bank. If I need to take a day off, I can, and there's no drama because I have a stockpile to turn to.

Your 'focussed work days' should be pure productivity. Have a think about where in your business you can start batching. Identify three areas of your business where you can batch create. Book some time in your diary for your batch days and go for it – get that stock-pile going – you won't regret it!

Element 2: Streamlining your business

If you have put all of the streamlined time tools in place, hopefully you will be feeling good and making massive progress. Now, we need to get your business to a similar place. I can't even begin to tell you how good your time and business will feel when you get started with streamlining and automation.

Before we go on, I want to highlight three different areas of my business which I streamlined, in the hope of helping you to identify what you can streamline.

Membership Management: My old system was messy and I needed a Customer Relationship Management (CRM) system. It was time to replace my spreadsheets as they had become inefficient. Getting a CRM in place meant I'd have all my important customer information organised and I could remove myself from time-consuming admin processes. Before my CRM system, I had to manually email all my members to see if they wanted to renew annually. I also had to chase failed payments. With a CRM, I could get all this done on autopilot! It was significant streamlining, as it gave me so much time back and it automated the process too.

My Email: This was a big one. I put my email boundary auto responder in place and took email off my phone. The major thing I realised with email was that I had a lot of very similar enquiry emails from people, so I knew I could streamline it. I crafted three template responses to common emails and stored them in my draft folder. So as the enquiries came in, I simply copied and pasted one of my canned responses. Such a simple win but, over the course of a year, imagine how much time it saved me! It's these little things we need to tease out of your business. Also unsubscribing from a ton of newsletters made my inbox feel less cluttered and overwhelming. I stopped replying to emails which didn't actually need a reply and just spent way less time in my inbox.

Processing Expenses: I always found collecting, keeping and processing all my receipts difficult. I would lose them, forget to save them, and they would stack up – and totally stress me out. I found it time-consuming reconciling them and it just wasn't an efficient use of my time, so I knew I needed to streamline this process. I did this by using some software called Receipt Bank, which integrated with an accounting system called Xero. I had the Receipt Bank app on my phone, which allowed me to photograph my receipts and upload them straight to Xero where they are automatically reconciled. Such a simple change saved me hours every month and gave me back some mental bandwidth.

If any of the above have sparked inspiration on what you can streamline, make a note. We will get down to some action in Element 4.

Element 3: Automation

Automation is really powerful and can help grow your business, even when you are not working on it. You are effectively replacing you and your time with automatic processes that require no intervention. We live in a time where there is technology for everything, and we can automate time-consuming things such as growing our email list, onboarding new members, handling failed payments and creating subscriptions instead of requesting payments etc. We can set our social posts to go out when we want and we can sell digital products on autopilot. There's SO much we can automate and it feels so good once it's set-up and in place.

Once I had my new CRM installed and I'd streamlined my membership processes, I was ready to automate. I want to give you three examples of how I use automation to gain more balance:

Growing my email list with potential customers, with a pre-written automated email sequence. People opted in via my website, which triggered the automated emails to them, offering them free value and for them to get to know me better, which in turn builds "know, like and trust".

Created a no-input-required membership onboarding process; this changed my life as I entirely removed myself from the long process! It was all automated via my CRM system and a membership plugin.

Using automation to recoup revenue. Using my CRM and email sequence to handle all failed payments via an automated email sequence, telling people how to update their card payments.

TRUTH BOMB: Where there's a will there's a way and there's always a way

These are just three ways I've used automation to make my business more efficient, profitable and easier to manage. My business really changed when I found Zapier too. If you use lots of different programmes like I do (PayPal, ActiveCampaign, AccessAlly, Stripe, Xero and others), you can create 'Zaps' which automate different programmes and software you use.

Have you had any 'a-ha' moments about where you can automate in your business? Make a note, because we will put it all together in Element 4.

Element 4: The Automation and Streamlining Audit

So, let's go back to your Clarity Plan in your workbook. We are going to start getting your business ship-shape and as slick as possible. We will go back to your recurring and repeatable tasks and, from there, look for anything that can be streamlined or automated to make your life easier. Simply write down on the audit page the processes from your Clarity Plan that, in an ideal world, you would streamline or automate. Having them on a fresh page and rewriting them will give us even more clarity around them, and we can see what we're working with more easily. Write down the process, then whether you are going to streamline or automate or, as with my CRM system, streamline and automate it in one. Next, we will create a wish list, in terms of solutions for streamlining and automation.

We also need to start thinking about what we can let go of mentally. As entrepreneurs, we tend to do as much as we can ourselves and hold on to tasks, when actually the smartest thing to do is to release our grip. There will be tasks where you think "I could NEVER let go of that" when, in fact, with a bit of journaling around your blocks, or just even thinking about how your business will look, you can let go of a lot. Commit to an easier way and you will be amazed how many limiting beliefs will fall by the wayside.

Once you've identified what you can streamline or automate, work out the steps you need to take to make it happen, then build them into your FAST lists. Think about research, budget and any support you might need. Doing this exercise and gaining clarity on where you can streamline and automate your business is a huge thing to do for yourself. I know this, because I'm living it. I am now reaping the rewards of spending the time to reorganise myself and my business. I had to do some journaling work on myself to learn to relinquish some control, but through little steps and keeping my focus, I was able to achieve this.

Action Step:

Once you have completed your clear streamlining and automation audit, create FASTS around the steps you need to take in order to make it all happen.

Let us know in the Face book Group, or tag me on Instagram @VictoriaKnowlesLacks, use #MakeItHappenBook, with what you are committing to streamlining, and any breakthroughs you have had.

Principle Six:

Outsourcing

"Are we limiting our success by not mastering the art of delegation? ...it's simply a matter of preparation meeting opportunity."
Oprah Winfrey

In Principle Six I want to share with you how to outsource effectively, in order to feel better and work on the things that light you up and drive you forward. Outsourcing is not only liberating, it's great for business to clear all of the tasks that you can't automate off your plate. In order to have a successful and balanced business, we need to get rid of the low value 'busy' work, in favour of working on the big things that drive revenue and align with our purpose. Doing everything yourself isn't cool, neither is focussing on all the £5 per hour tasks, when your focus and attention should be on the £500 + tasks.

Principle Six – Outcomes:

- Identifying the tasks and jobs that we can outsource
- Creating a plan to outsource
- Finding the right people

Outsourcing is the perfect answer for tasks that are not in your skill set, that you find difficult or just don't really want to do, because let's be honest, there are some tasks we all don't want to do. When done right, outsourcing is an essential part of growth and it supercharges productivity as we're clearing the decks.

When you let go of tasks that hold you down and keep you busy, you start to flourish. Often your best ideas come forward and you start to do your best work. You become more content and this is what we're aiming for!

I want to talk to you about what I call "skilling up", which is outsourcing to experts. It's utilising people who have expertise in areas where we don't. It enables us to close skills gaps in our businesses and have a job very well done – instead of just about done – by us.

Example

I wanted to run my membership with a plugin called AccessAlly on The Ladies Shooting Club website. Websites aren't in my area of expertise. I know my way around Wordpress on a basic level, but plugins just aren't in my zone of genius and it would have taken me days to get to grips with. I could have integrated that plugin, but it wouldn't have been done properly, so I would have had to get expert help in anyway. To save potential headaches, time and potentially hashing up my website, I skilled up and hired in some help. I found a wonderful tech lady who was an expert in that Plugin. She did what I needed, and set up some bonus processes and features that I didn't even know about – the results were excellent.

Where in your business do you have these massive frustrations and roadblocks? Maybe it's in Facebook Ads, Website Tech, Accounting, Marketing or Manufacturing? Just have a think about where you need some help.

Remember in Part One, I held onto all my tasks for as long as I could and wore my busy as a badge of honour? I was unknowingly choking my business, because I was trying to do it all myself.

You might be thinking, *"This all sounds amazing Victoria, but I can't possibly let someone else do something in my business! What if they mess it up?!"* To some entrepreneurs, delegating or outsourcing tasks is terrifying – I see this a lot. To many of us, our businesses are our babies and the thought of someone else doing parts of our work we've always done can freak us out. We have to get over this if we really want to grow.

TRUTH BOMB: You can't lead a balanced life, or do your best work when you are trying to do everything yourself

Imagine if you spent most of your working day in your Genius Zone, just doing what you are good at – working on all those things you thought you'd be doing every day when you started your business? Seriously, how good would that feel? These are the things you hardly ever get to do, when reality hits – as do all the tasks in which you become caught up. It's a matter of pure productivity and just getting great work done. You are not rushed, not pushed and doing work you care about. Therefore, you must outsource! I remember thinking: "Do I want to be spending summer afternoons doing my book- keeping or do I want to be out in the sunshine with my family?" This got me thinking: Does it really matter if I don't schedule my own social media? Does it really matter if someone else is editing my videos? When all is said and done, does it matter? No, of course it doesn't.

What are your strengths?

Do you know your strengths? When we do, we can play to them and really drive our businesses forward. I know it's obvious, but if you are a strong designer but a lousy book keeper, then your time needs to be spent creating beautiful designs. If bookkeeping takes you days and makes you lose the will, then you need to outsource this to someone who has a passion for figures. When you have your passion and play to your strengths, that's really where the magic happens.

Quick Win: Not sure of your strengths? Create a little Facebook poll, ask a few of your nearest and dearest what they think you are good at.

You might be thinking *"I can't afford to pay anyone!"* Trust me, I know this feeling. In the early days of my business, I couldn't afford to pay myself, let alone anyone else. Can you do a skill swap to begin with, or perhaps barter? This is a call you must make.

Do you invest a small amount on £5 an hour tasks, to allow you to be free to work on your £500 an hour tasks? The answer to this should be "yes" every time. It will allow you to get rid of the small 'busy' stuff, so you can work on the things you love – and that all-important revenue generation.

Is there anything in your £5 an hour list that you can actually let go of to make your life easier? You might find as your business grows there are things that just aren't as important and not business critical.

When you are starting out and money is tight and you don't have the money to spend on freelancers, it can be difficult. When you adopt a growth mindset, however, you will always find the answers, even if things sometimes seem impossible.

Remember when my Mum used to help me with the memberships, or when friends would step in and host events to give me my Saturdays back? Have a look at Freelancers and virtual assistants by the hour. They can take on some of your work for a small cost.

During the early days I couldn't afford a virtual assistant, so I had two amazing interns from a local university, and I had an apprentice. This was a great way of getting my £5 an hour tasks done and, at the same time, provided valuable work experience for some bright and keen students. I also outsourced to a great lady in Malaysia I found on Fiverr. She was so lovely and the quality of her work was incredible.

Hopefully you are with me on the power of outsourcing, and that you can see how fundamental it is to balance. Outsourcing is also so important to growth, and even to our happiness too. I am excited for you to take some action and to start thinking outsourcing.

Action Time!

We are going to get really clear on the things that you can out-source. The time might be right now, or it might be in the not-too-distant future. Either way, being prepared is going to benefit you.

Here's what we're going to do:

- Revisit your Clarity Plan in Principle Two. Find the recurring tasks you put a value on, paying attention to those low value tasks in particular.
- Take some time to go through the list and have a serious think about what you can outsource. There will be things you can outsource immediately, but others will be slow-burners for now.
- In your workbook, on the outsourcing page, write your top five things that can be outsourced. Include your £5 and any £50 per hour tasks. These are the things that take you ages, but could take someone else half the time – those things that fill you with dread, and those you just want to stop doing!
- Think about your budget and plan accordingly. What can you afford to outsource now? What will have to wait a while?
- Research possible people to whom you could out-source your tasks. Think about people who are in your network. Look at outsourcing / freelancer web-sites such as Fiverr, PeopleperHour and Upwork. Has a friend recommended someone? Find someone who you can afford, who you 'click' with and, most im-portantly, trust.
- Think about how you need to prepare for outsourc-ing. What does the person need to know? What's the scope of the role? What are your expectations from them? What is the timeline? How will it look? Will you create a step-by-step Google Doc for them?

Think about a contract or signed agreement too. How about GDPR? These are all things which don't take long, but could be time consuming if you don't get them right. List some bullet points in your workbook so, when the time comes, you just have to join the dots and know you have everything.

TRUTH BOMB: The thing about outsourcing isn't that it costs us money, but that it brings us freedom and space. Space to up level our income and our daily life, too. If you are struggling to see this, it's definitely something to journal to find your reasons why

Here are some examples of things I outsourced and how I did it:

- Scheduling social media posts (Twitter, Instagram and Facebook).

I have the most wonderful social media guy, James from 'Knowing Media, Knowing You'. He took over all my business social profiles and schedules a week's worth of content at a time. I email him on a Monday morning with my goals for that week and he does the rest. I spend around £100 per week on social media, which I calculate to save me about £1,000 worth of time every week, as I'm freed up to work on bigger picture goals.

- Creating social posts from templates in Canva.

I have a solid brand with a set colour scheme, look and fonts. So, I created a few templates in Canva and wrote what I was looking for and my social media guy gave it a go. He produced some outstanding results as part of his workload for me and took the entire thing off my plate. The time I save from getting lost in Canva and social media gives me a few hours a week back to just chill and do what I want to do.

- Uploading web copy and formatting web pages.

I'm not the most tech savvy person out there. WordPress just isn't in my Genius Zone. In the past, I've spent hours trying to make posts look fancy, but I become waylaid, the formatting looks wrong and it makes me mad. My solution to this was finding a brilliant freelancer for £10 per web post on PeoplePerHour.com. I use the same girl all the time. I send the direction, images and text, and she works her magic!

- Sending event emails.

Anyone can do this. Even though my name is at the bottom of the email which goes to event guests, the email is copied and pasted with just the location, time and date changed. Pip (my gorgeous friend who sadly died) used to do these emails for me every week, which saved me hours and was invaluable. Now, the S&CBC Regional Officers do their own for their events.

- Posting members' badges.

I used to write a handwritten card with every single member's badge. Then it became too much as I would have renewals every day and I became stressed out about it. Now, I send all the badges out to everyone in one go. I have a printed card which goes in with the badge. I pay my sister to help me fill envelopes and print addresses. What was two weeks' worth of work in sending everyone a badge at the same time, is now taken off my plate and costs me less than £200!

Can you see how, by farming out these £5 per hour tasks, I've really gained a lot of time back? There were a lot more tasks too before I regionalised the S&CBC. You really have to let the little things go in order to make big strides forward in business.

So, hopefully you are feeling super excited about the potential of what you can let go of and where your can put your focus in a more positive way. When you outsource, you can really drive things forward and create some precious space. The key I found with out-sourcing was to be prepared; this will save you a lot of time in the long run.

If outsourcing is not working out, then bring it back in. If you have a person in place who isn't the right fit, that's ok; sometimes you have to kiss a few frogs in business. Thank them for their service and move on. By knowing what you don't want, you make way for what you do.

Are you ready to outsource? From the exercise you have just completed, let us know your takeaways, or anything you are committing to outsource in the MAKE IT HAPPEN // MINDSET AND MOTIVATION // THE BOOK Facebook Group. Or, as always, tag me in a post on Instagram and use #MakeItHappenBook

Principle Seven: Maintaining Balance

"Time and balance are the two most difficult things to have control over, yet they are both the things that we do control."
Catherine Pulsifer.

Principle Seven is all about maintenance and staying on track. We can have the best will in the world and be super organised by following the previous six Principles to the letter but, in life, we all get curveballs and challenges we have to deal with that come out of the blue.

This Principle is about having effective strategies in place and staying on track. For me it has been all about the right perspective and approach and knowing that it's not what happens to us, but how we let it affect us that can give or take away balance. It is about letting go sometimes, being flexible and creating practices to retain harmony in your business.

Principle Seven Outcomes:

- Utilising the mindset tools
- The 'knowing' that everything always works out
- Feeling your feelings
- Identifying and managing curveballs
- Creating actions for reactions
- Saying goodbye to stress and worry. Managing your time (and evaluating it).
- Reminding yourself. You will find your own path to staying balanced as you go and

- figure out what works for you and what doesn't – it's all part of the process

Principle Seven is about inspiring and reminding you – think of it as your maintenance Principle.

I love that you have got this far and I am so excited for you to get the changes in your life that I have had. I know that if you stick to the daily practice and the Seven Principles of Balance, you will change your life and your business. A balanced business and lifestyle is not a quick win; it's a constant investment of time in yourself. A big part of it is keeping the faith that everything will work out.

By now, hopefully you feel you have the tools you need to get started and start making amazing, positive changes. Little steps are what it's all about and I know first-hand that little steps add up to big, life changing strides. Keeping balance is all about keeping perspective. When you know this, you can put anything into context and then reframe it to something more positive.

With perspective, you can let go of things which don't really matter: things like what people have done or said which have hurt or upset you. From a place of perspective, you can be grateful for the lessons you learn and the clarity you gain. When you have clarity, you have a plan and, from a plan, you have a clear route for action. When you take action, you achieve, when you achieve, you feel good. When you are consistently going in the right direction, you form new habits. I hope all the mindset tools and Principles will change your life, just like they did for me.

I want to share a realisation with you that I had not long ago. It was that I actually have all of the answers within me, in terms of moving forward and next steps. When I realised this, I committed to it and sought to find the next steps from within and trust myself. This has been really powerful, especially in writing this book. Finding the answers will likely take a fair bit of trial and error but, ultimately, they are there. Whatever it is that feels so impossible to you now, deep down you know what to do – please remember that.

I don't have instructions on how you find your answers but, for me, it all started with keeping the faith that situations will evolve and ultimately improve. and being confident in that.

TRUTH BOMB: Giving up is never rewarded – courage and keeping going always is

I genuinely believe that everything comes down to feelings, and the sooner you can get some positive momentum, gratitude and happiness going, the better your life will be. If you are having a bad day, you have the power to change it. If someone has upset you or wronged you, think about what that has triggered inside of you.

You don't have to stay in a bad mood for long and you don't always have to be right. To me, happiness is more important, going about my day and striving towards what I want to achieve. When you feel out of balance, bring on that grateful feeling and reframe it.

By feeling grateful, chances are you will deal with things in a totally different way, and not let things spiral from bad to worse – you will just move on. Don't underestimate the power of your feelings and how you react. Be aware how outcomes differ based on your mood.

Our feelings, moods and outlook all have a big part to play in the day-to-day, which ultimately affect the quality of our lives. For example, the classic 'getting out of bed the wrong side', is commonly blamed when we start the day in a bad mood, and we can often have a less than ideal day and attract all the bad vibes. This is the same on the flip side too. When we wake up feeling grateful and in a good mood, like will attract like and the better we will feel, the more our RAS will bring it to us, and the more positive momentum will build. In that state of joy, you can't help but feel great and as if you can do anything!

Just knowing you can turn it around is really powerful. Can you now see how you have a choice? Succumb to self-pity or gloom, or switch it around to joy? Now you have the mindset tools such as perspective, reframing, journaling and your morning routine, you can start to cultivate more positivity.

Habits are just repeated thoughts that become automatic, so if you have a habit of seeing the worst in everything, you can now re-write that by flooding your conscious mind with positivity and possibility. This will, of course, be easier for some people, and for me it was easy as I was ready. The fact is it is more than possible, it is absolutely doable with the mindset tools and your morning routine. Will it be easy? If you make it so. Will you be perfect every day? No, of course you won't, but a few steps forward and a step back will be ok, as you will be heading in the right direction.

TRUTH BOMB: Everyone has the power to change when they open their mind to it

A big part of balance and positivity is the need to stay flexible. There will be days where it all feels hopeless, but those days will pass and, instead of self-sabotaging, just take deep breaths, see the good, learn the lessons and keep moving forward. Nothing is ultimately ever that bad – even when the worst thing possible happens, we can learn from it.

Be flexible with yourself and your business, whether it is in terms of your FASTs, your day, your boundaries, your expectations, people, and time. Do what you can with what you have, and know that is all you can do. Beating yourself up or being too rigid with yourself is a sure-fire way to invite stress in and fall off the wagon. I totally understand that there are times, though, when situations can get the better of us, and it seems like flexibility just won't cut it.

We know our energy is precious and it needs guarding, so if we can protect it then we should. To me, that has meant identifying those downward spiral situations, which I call 'Curveballs'. When we identify them, we can make a plan to manage them and not give them the focus we once might have. When we do that, they lose their power, we preserve our energy and remain focussed on what actually matters to us. Curveballs seem to come at the most inconvenient of times, and usually bring a fair amount of stress and drama with them, but they also bring us growth – which is golden – so do try and bear that in mind.

Examples of Curveballs:

- An argument or clashing with someone.
- Getting a negative or inflammatory comment on social media.
- Someone being rude to you unnecessarily.
- Someone sapping your time.

In all these situations, it is all about changing our reaction. Yes, they are all annoying and can be hurtful, but we need stop the negative feelings before they escalate. By identifying our curveballs, we can create some 'Action for Reaction' strategies, which will allow us to move on quicker and not get sucked into a downward spiral. There are pre-planned reframing points to refer to – like a safety net for your mood. By pre-empting your reaction, you are better equipped and can move on quicker.

Here is an example:

Situation: Clashing with someone you care about (friend / family member etc).

Old Reaction: Anger. Wanting to have the last word. Blame. Wanting to show them you are right. Insecurity. Telling other friends (which perpetuates the negative feelings, which actually makes the situation bigger, creates a divide and leads to more animosity). Wanting to cut them off etc.

New Reaction: Compassion. Resolve. Moving on swiftly. You may know you are right, but your relationship is worth more than being right. Make allowances for them if you need to (maybe they have a lot going on). Make your happiness a priority over being right. Let go of wanting to be right.

Action: Close down the conversation on a positive note. Refuse to be sucked in further. Walk away. In your head, list five reasons why you love them as a friend. Journal why you feel you are right, and then tell yourself to release it. Meditate, or listen to a song that makes you smile. Sometimes you must be the bigger person and keep in mind the bigger picture. What is more important, your relationship or being right?

Don't Worry, Be Happy

Worrying is not conducive to balance and we need to let go of as much of it as possible. In this context, I am talking about stress-based, mindless worrying and low-level anxiety – where we just worry on autopilot. I know this isn't something you can just turn off, but we absolutely can manage it. When you are worrying about something, remember to ask yourself: *"Where is the proof?"* Keep asking yourself this until you have no proof, or maybe try acting like someone who doesn't have a care in the world – and see what happens! So much that we worry about never actually happens. We are conditioned to go into 'fight or flight' mode and can become addicted to that chemical release of cortisol – and therefore addicted to drama!

Remembering it all!

So, now we know how, we just need to remember it all and create reminders to keep putting all of this into action!
Here are my top five quick wins for remembering it all:

1.   **Recurring phone reminders:** These are such a quick and effective strategy and I have five daily phone reminders that pop up throughout the day. They can be inspiring quotations, fun emojis, or self-care prompts – anything that resonates with you. You can change these as often as you like.
     Note: Keep your phone on silent when you are working, even if it's just for an hour.
2.   **Inspirational screensavers:** These are a fun way to stay connected to things that motivate and inspire you. I have an inspirational vision board set as the background on my laptop. It has elements of things I

want to achieve, and things that calm me.

3.   **Actual notes:** Write out little reminder post-it notes. Stick them on your mirror, your toilet door, on the dashboard in your car – anywhere!

4.   **Accountability**: Get someone to have a weekly check-in with, to see how balanced and on track you are. Having someone to hold us accountable is so powerful, and the motivation of not wanting to look bad is really effective! Use our Facebook Group or find someone who will be honest with you.

5.   **Committing every single day:** Commit to following what you have learnt, and just remember that you weren't born to play small. Love hard, be kind to yourself and others, and do the work to achieve your best possible life.

For one last time, let us know your takeaways in the MAKE IT HAPPEN // MINDSET AND MOTIVATION // THE BOOK Facebook Group or tag me, @VictoriaKnowlesLacks on Instagram or use the hashtag #MakeItHappenBook!

I love that you have been through my journey with me, and I am excited for you to start yours. I love that you have read all the way to the end, and hope you have lots of takeaways, and are ready to change the game for yourself. You simply do not need to burn out to be successful. Far from it, you just need the commitment to succeed, alongside structure, and the right approach. Let's all commit to making it happen, on our terms, having space around us, working less, making more impact and living more.

If you need more help with mindset or balance in your business, then do visit my website www.victoriaknowleslacks.com and see how we can work together, plus I have some digital products which I think you'll love.

Keep a journal to look back on a year from now, and see how your life has changed. Let go of more stuff and see how your life changes. Keep in touch with me in the MAKE IT HAPPEN // MINDSET AND MOTIVATION // THE BOOK Facebook Group.

I have so much faith in you.

I know you can do anything.

Just go for it and make it happen!